WHAT REALLY CHANGED THE WORLD

EXPLORING THE TECHNOLOGICAL EVOLUTION OF HUMANITY

SANDEEP CHAVAN

GYRUS
VISION

CONTENTS

PREFACE
1: INTRODUCTION
2: UNDERSTANDING TECHNOLOGY
3: ARTIFICIAL INTELLIGENCE AND MACHINE LEARNING
4: BLOCKCHAIN TECHNOLOGY
5: INTERNET OF THINGS (IOT)
6: AUGMENTED AND VIRTUAL REALITY
7: BIOTECHNOLOGY AND GENETIC ENGINEERING
8: RENEWABLE ENERGY TECHNOLOGIES
9: ADVANCED ROBOTICS
10: 3D PRINTING
11: SPACE EXPLORATION TECHNOLOGIES
12: CYBERSECURITY INNOVATIONS
13: FUTURE TECHNOLOGIES AND TRENDS
14: FOSTERING INNOVATION AND ENTREPRENEURSHIP
15: CONCLUSION
ACKNOWLEDGMENTS
ABOUT THE AUTHOR
REFERENCES
MESSAGE TO READERS

PREFACE

What Really Changed The World: Exploring the Technological Evolution of Humanity is a book born out of my deep curiosity and passion for understanding how human ingenuity has shaped the world we live in. Technology, in its many forms, is not just a collection of tools, machines, or systems; it represents the boundless creativity of the human mind and our drive to solve the problems we face as a species. From the invention of the wheel to the rise of artificial intelligence, we have witnessed incredible innovations that have not only transformed society but also redefined what it means to be human.

This book is written with one specific audience in mind: the young, curious minds of India and beyond. As an educator and engineer, I have often come across students eager to explore, create, and innovate, but unsure of where to begin or how to think about the complex technologies that dominate our world today. It is my hope that this book will serve as a guide—a starting point—for young innovators, helping them understand the historical context of technological breakthroughs, their global impact, and the future possibilities they offer.

Each chapter of this book covers a pivotal technology, tracing its development from its origins to the present day, while also providing a glimpse into the future. But this book is not just about technical knowledge. At its core, it's about inspiration. I want the readers to see the vast potential of human intelligence, to understand that our capacity to innovate is limitless. And yet, with great power comes great responsibility. Technology is a double-edged sword—it can be used for progress and prosperity, but it can also cause destruction if misused. I have devoted considerable attention to the ethical dilemmas we face today, urging readers to think critically about how we shape the future.

As we stand on the cusp of incredible advancements, from artificial intelligence to biotechnology, my message is simple: the future is in your hands. It is up to you, the next generation, to wield the tools of technology wisely, to create solutions that uplift humanity, and to ensure that the innovations of tomorrow serve the greater good.

I would like to express my gratitude to the many scientists, engineers, entrepreneurs, and visionaries whose work has made this book possible. I also want to thank my students, who have been my constant source of inspiration. Their questions, insights, and enthusiasm for learning have driven me to explore the intersection of technology and human values in this book.

I hope this book will spark your imagination, challenge your thinking, and most importantly, encourage you to pursue your own innovative ideas. The world needs new ideas, new inventions, and new solutions—and it is my firm belief that you are the ones who will bring them to life.

Er Sandeep Chavan
Author and Educator

1: INTRODUCTION

Significance of Technology in Shaping Society

Technology has been a cornerstone of human advancement throughout history. From the invention of the wheel to the development of the internet, each technological leap has fundamentally altered how societies function, communicate, and evolve. The relationship between technology and society is symbiotic; as technology advances, it reshapes social structures, cultural norms, and economic frameworks.

Historical Impact

1. **Early Innovations**:
   - The wheel, one of humanity's earliest technological advancements, facilitated trade and transportation, leading to increased economic activity and cultural exchange.
   - The advent of agriculture allowed humans to settle in one place, forming communities, leading to the rise of civilizations.

2. **The Industrial Revolution**:
   - Marked a significant turning point where mechanization changed the landscape of work, moving societies from agrarian economies to industrial powerhouses.
   - Innovations such as the steam engine and the spinning jenny revolutionized production, enabling mass manufacturing and urbanization.

3. **The Digital Age**:
   - The late 20th century saw the rise of computers and the internet, leading to the

- information age.
- Technology began to influence nearly every aspect of life—from how we communicate (social media) to how we conduct business (e-commerce).

Contemporary Significance

Today, technology drives globalization, enhances connectivity, and provides platforms for social change. The rapid development of artificial intelligence, biotechnology, and renewable energy is shaping our present and will significantly influence our future.

1. **Globalization**:
   - Technology has bridged geographical divides, allowing for instant communication and collaboration across borders.
   - The rise of multinational corporations and global markets has created interdependence among nations.

2. **Social Change**:
   - Movements like #MeToo and Black Lives Matter have utilized technology to raise awareness and mobilize support.
   - The role of technology in democratizing information has empowered individuals and communities.

3. **Economic Growth**:
   - Innovative technologies have the potential to drive economic growth, creating new industries and job opportunities.
   - Startups and entrepreneurs leverage technology to disrupt traditional markets, fostering a culture of innovation.

Objective of the Book:

Inspiring Young Innovators

The objective of this book is to explore the technological evolution of humanity and to inspire young innovators, particularly in India, to engage with these advancements. As we stand on the brink of unprecedented change, it is essential to cultivate a mindset of innovation and adaptability.

Why Focus on Young Innovators?

1. **Future Leaders**:
   - Today's youth are tomorrow's leaders. Equipping them with knowledge about cutting-edge technologies is crucial for fostering a new generation of thinkers, creators, and problem solvers.
   - Encouraging young minds to innovate can drive societal progress and address pressing global challenges.

2. **Global Competitiveness**:
   - As India aims to become a global leader in technology and innovation, nurturing the skills and creativity of young people is vital.
   - This book seeks to provide them with insights into the latest technological trends, encouraging them to contribute to the global dialogue.

3. **Empowerment through Knowledge**:
   - By understanding the historical context and future implications of technology, young readers can develop critical thinking and analytical skills.
   - The book aims to empower them to envision their role in the technological landscape, encouraging them to take initiative and pursue their ideas.

Structure of the Book

Each subsequent chapter will delve into a specific technology, tracing its historical development, current global applications, and future potential. By exploring these themes, the book will offer a comprehensive view of how technology has transformed our world and how young innovators can harness these advancements for positive change.

The narrative will include:

- Historical anecdotes and case studies to illustrate key points.
- Global perspectives that highlight different countries' contributions and challenges.
- Insights and quotes from industry leaders and innovators to inspire readers.

In conclusion, this chapter sets the stage for a journey through the technological evolution of humanity, emphasizing the importance of technology in shaping our societies and the vital role that young innovators will play in the future. By understanding the past and present, we can collectively forge a brighter tomorrow.

2: UNDERSTANDING TECHNOLOGY

Historical Context: From the Wheel to the Internet

1. The Beginnings of Technology: Primitive Tools and Early Inventions

The journey of technology began with simple tools crafted from stone, bone, and wood. These tools, developed by early humans, marked the beginning of humanity's technological evolution. The first axes, spears, and fire-starting techniques allowed our ancestors to hunt, gather, and eventually establish communities. Over thousands of years, these rudimentary technologies laid the foundation for more complex systems.

Key Milestones:

- **Stone Tools (~2.6 million years ago)**: The first recorded technology, stone tools allowed early humans to process food and perform basic tasks. These tools laid the groundwork for survival and development.
- **Fire (~1.7 million years ago)**: Mastery over fire was a crucial development in early human history, providing warmth, protection, and the ability to cook food. Fire also extended human activity into the night and opened the door to metallurgy much later.

2. The Invention of the Wheel (circa 3500 BC)

The invention of the wheel was one of the most groundbreaking moments in human history. Originating in Mesopotamia, the wheel revolutionized transportation, enabling humans to move goods, people, and resources over long distances. While initially used for pottery, it soon became integral to the creation of carts, enabling trade and communication between civilizations.

Impact:

- **Trade Expansion**: The wheel facilitated long-distance trade, connecting different civilizations and enabling the exchange of goods and ideas. This contributed to the cultural and technological enrichment of societies.

- **Agricultural Efficiency**: The invention of the wheel also influenced the development of farming tools and transportation, allowing farmers to manage larger tracts of land and produce surplus crops.

3. The Industrial Revolution (18th Century)

The 18th century witnessed a technological revolution that transformed the world— the Industrial Revolution. This period marked a dramatic shift from manual labor to mechanized processes. Steam engines, textile machines, and iron production innovations allowed industries to mass-produce goods, fostering urbanization and creating new economic opportunities.

Key Inventions:

- **The Steam Engine**: James Watt's improvements to the steam engine in the late 18th century played a pivotal role in industrialization. The steam engine became the power source behind factories, trains, and ships, accelerating production and transportation.
- **Textile Machines**: Innovations like the spinning jenny and the power loom transformed the textile industry, increasing production speed and lowering costs. This shift to mechanized textile production helped establish the factory system.

Impact:

- **Global Economic Growth**: The Industrial Revolution catalyzed the creation of modern economies. Nations with advanced technologies, like the UK and later the US, experienced rapid economic growth, while other countries followed suit.
- **Urbanization**: Mechanized industry required labor, leading to the growth of cities as people moved from rural areas to work in factories.

4. The Digital Revolution (20th Century)

The latter half of the 20th century witnessed the rise of digital technologies that would redefine nearly every aspect of human life. The development of computers and the birth of the internet created a networked world, ushering in the Information Age.

Key Developments:
- **Computers**: Starting with early machines like ENIAC (1945), computers evolved from massive, room-sized machines to personal devices. The development of microprocessors, pioneered by companies like Intel, allowed for computers to become smaller, more powerful, and affordable for everyday use.
- **The Internet (1960s-1990s)**: Originally developed as a military communication system (ARPANET), the internet rapidly grew into a global network for sharing information. Tim Berners-Lee's invention of the World Wide Web (1989) brought the internet into homes, businesses, and classrooms, transforming the way we communicate, learn, and work.

Impact:
- **Global Connectivity**: The internet created a global village where people, businesses, and governments could interact in real-time, regardless of geographic location. This connectivity spurred economic globalization and cross-cultural exchange.
- **The Information Economy**: The rise of digital technologies created new industries, from e-commerce to cloud computing, shifting the global economy towards services and knowledge-based industries.

Global Contributions to Technological Evolution

While technological advancements are often associated with specific countries or regions, the reality is that progress has been a cumulative effort by civilizations and cultures across the globe.

1. Mesopotamia: The Birthplace of Civilization and Early Technology

As one of the world's first civilizations, Mesopotamia laid the foundation for many technological innovations. In addition to the wheel, Mesopotamians developed writing systems (cuneiform), mathematics, and irrigation techniques, all of which were critical to the development of human society.

Key Contributions:

- **Mathematics and Astronomy**: Mesopotamians devised early mathematical systems, including the concept of zero. Their understanding of astronomy also led to the creation of the first calendars.
- **Irrigation**: Mesopotamians engineered complex irrigation systems to control the Tigris and Euphrates rivers, enabling large-scale agriculture and the growth of cities.

2. China: Pioneers in Innovation

China has a rich history of technological innovation, much of which had a profound impact on global development. From paper-making and printing to gunpowder and the compass, Chinese inventions played a central role in global trade, warfare, and culture.

Key Contributions:

- **Paper and Printing**: The Chinese invention of paper (circa 105 AD) revolutionized communication and record-keeping. Later, the development of movable-type printing during the Song Dynasty (960–1279 AD) enabled mass production of texts, spreading knowledge across the world.
- **The Compass**: The Chinese developed the magnetic compass in the 11th century, which was essential for navigation and played a pivotal role in global exploration.

3. The Islamic Golden Age: A Hub of Knowledge and Invention

During the Islamic Golden Age (8th to 14th centuries), scholars and inventors made significant contributions to science, mathematics, medicine, and engineering. Islamic civilizations acted as a bridge between ancient knowledge and the Renaissance, preserving and expanding upon Greek, Roman, and Persian scientific traditions.

Key Contributions:

- **Algebra and Algorithms**: The mathematician Al-Khwarizmi, often referred to as the "father of algebra," introduced concepts that would become the basis for modern mathematics and computer science.
- **Medicine**: Scholars like Ibn Sina (Avicenna) wrote extensively on medicine, compiling medical knowledge that influenced European and Asian practices for centuries.

4. Europe: The Age of Exploration and Industrialization

The Renaissance and Enlightenment periods in Europe brought about a resurgence in scientific inquiry, leading to discoveries in physics, astronomy, and biology. European inventors and scientists like Galileo, Isaac Newton, and Leonardo da Vinci laid the groundwork for modern science and engineering.

Key Contributions:

- **The Scientific Method**: European scientists formalized the scientific method, which became the foundation for modern empirical research and technological development.
- **Industrial Innovation**: The Industrial Revolution, which began in Britain, rapidly spread across Europe and North America, transforming agriculture, industry, and transportation.

5. India: Ancient Innovation and Modern Technological Powerhouse

India has been a center of innovation for millennia, with significant contributions to mathematics, astronomy, and metallurgy. In recent decades, India has emerged as a global leader in IT and space technologies, contributing to the global technological landscape.

Key Contributions:

- **Mathematics**: Ancient Indian mathematicians, such as Aryabhata and Brahmagupta, were pioneers in algebra and astronomy, introducing concepts like zero and the decimal system.
- **Modern IT Revolution**: India's rise as a global IT hub in the 21st century has been fueled by its vast talent pool and technological infrastructure, with companies like Infosys, TCS, and Wipro becoming global players.

6. The United States: The Technological Superpower of the 20th and 21st Century

The 20th and 21st centuries have seen the United States at the forefront of technological innovation, particularly in computing, aerospace, and biotechnology. Major developments in Silicon Valley, including personal computers, the internet, and social media, have reshaped the global economy and culture.

Key Contributions:

- **The Internet and Personal Computing**: Innovators like Steve Jobs, Bill Gates, and Tim Berners-Lee revolutionized the way the world communicates, learns, and conducts business.
- **Space Exploration**: NASA's space programs have pushed the boundaries of human exploration, from landing on the moon to missions on Mars.

Conclusion: A Collective Human Effort

The development of technology is not limited to one region or culture. It is a collective effort involving countless individuals, civilizations, and societies. As the world continues to evolve, understanding this shared history of innovation is crucial. The future of technology will be built on the foundations laid by the inventors, scientists, and dreamers who came before us. The next chapters will dive deeper into specific technologies that are shaping our modern world and the role of future innovators in driving technological progress.

3: ARTIFICIAL INTELLIGENCE AND MACHINE LEARNING

Historical Development

1. The Early Roots of Artificial Intelligence

The concept of artificial intelligence (AI) dates back much earlier than one might think. Although AI as we know it began to take shape in the mid-20th century, the fascination with intelligent machines can be traced to ancient myths and early philosophical questions about the nature of thought and intelligence.

- **Ancient Myths and Philosophical Foundations**: Early ideas about intelligent creations appear in ancient Greek mythology, such as Hephaestus, the god of craftsmanship, who was said to have created mechanical servants. Throughout history, philosophers like Aristotle pondered whether human reasoning could be mechanized, laying a foundation for the exploration of artificial cognition.
- **Early Computational Models**: The real technological journey toward AI began in the 19th century with the work of mathematician and logician Charles Babbage. His design of the Analytical Engine, a theoretical general-purpose computer, laid the groundwork for programmable machines. Later, in the 1940s, Alan Turing proposed the idea of a machine that could simulate any human logic process, giving birth to the concept of a "universal machine." Turing's work on algorithms and his famous Turing Test, which evaluated a machine's ability to exhibit intelligent behavior indistinguishable from that of a human, are central to AI's intellectual roots.

2. The Birth of AI: The 1950s and 1960s

Artificial Intelligence as a formal field of study emerged in the 1950s. At a conference at Dartmouth College in 1956, computer scientist John McCarthy coined the term "artificial intelligence." The goal of AI research was initially clear: to create machines that could mimic human intelligence.

- **Early Milestones**: In the 1950s, Allen Newell and Herbert Simon developed the "Logic Theorist," one of the first AI programs, capable of solving complex mathematical problems. Soon after, Arthur Samuel created the first self-learning program—a checkers-playing machine that improved its skills by playing against itself.
- **The Rise of Symbolic AI**: Early AI focused on symbolic reasoning, where intelligence was thought to arise from manipulating symbols and following predefined rules. These systems, known as "rule-based" or "expert systems," dominated AI research for several decades. They performed well in specific, narrow domains, such as medical diagnostics or game playing, but struggled with real-world complexity.

3. AI Winter and the Shift to Machine Learning (1980s-2000s)

The AI field faced significant challenges by the 1970s and 1980s. The limitations of early AI systems—mainly their inability to deal with ambiguity and real-world variability—led to a period known as the "AI winter," where funding and interest in AI research declined.

- **Machine Learning Revolution**: In the late 1990s and early 2000s, the focus of AI research shifted toward machine learning, a subfield of AI that emphasizes teaching machines to learn from data rather than rely on explicit programming. Key breakthroughs included neural networks and statistical models that allowed machines to identify patterns and make decisions based on experience.

- **The Emergence of Deep Learning**: By the late 2000s, deep learning, a subset of machine learning that uses large neural networks, started to show promising results. Leveraging the growth in computational power and vast amounts of data, deep learning algorithms became capable of performing complex tasks like image recognition and language translation. This was demonstrated by the success of programs like Google DeepMind's AlphaGo, which defeated the world champion in the complex game of Go in 2016.

Global Impact and Applications
1. Artificial Intelligence in Everyday Life

AI is now an integral part of our daily lives, often in ways we might not even realize. From smartphones to smart homes, AI-driven applications have seamlessly integrated into the fabric of modern society.

- **Virtual Assistants**: AI-powered virtual assistants like Siri, Google Assistant, and Alexa use natural language processing to understand and respond to voice commands. They can perform tasks ranging from setting reminders to controlling home appliances, creating a personalized and interactive user experience.
- **Recommendation Systems**: AI is responsible for curating the content we see online, from personalized recommendations on streaming platforms like Netflix to product suggestions on e-commerce sites like Amazon. These recommendation systems use machine learning algorithms to analyze user behavior and preferences, optimizing engagement.

2. Transforming Industries

AI is revolutionizing entire industries, transforming how companies operate, innovate, and deliver products or services. The following sectors are experiencing particularly profound impacts:

- **Healthcare**: AI is enhancing diagnostic accuracy, predictive healthcare, and personalized medicine. Machine learning algorithms can analyze vast amounts of medical data, identifying patterns and early signs of diseases like cancer. AI-powered robots assist in surgeries, and systems like IBM Watson help clinicians make data-driven treatment decisions.
- **Transportation**: Autonomous vehicles, driven by AI systems, are set to transform transportation. Companies like Tesla and Waymo are developing self-driving cars that rely on AI to navigate roads, detect objects, and make split-second decisions in real time. These vehicles have the potential to reduce traffic accidents, improve fuel efficiency, and reshape urban planning.
- **Finance**: AI is transforming the financial industry by automating processes like fraud detection, risk assessment, and algorithmic trading. AI-powered systems analyze vast datasets in real time, making quicker and more accurate decisions than humans could. Robo-advisors are using AI to manage portfolios, providing cost-effective financial advice to individuals.
- **Manufacturing and Supply Chain**: AI is driving the fourth industrial revolution (Industry 4.0), where smart factories use AI to automate processes, optimize production lines, and predict equipment failures before they occur. AI-enabled robots work alongside humans to increase efficiency and precision in complex manufacturing tasks.

3. AI's Role in Social and Global Challenges

Beyond industrial applications, AI holds the potential to address some of the most pressing global challenges.

- **Climate Change and Sustainability**: AI is being applied to model and mitigate the effects of climate change.

Machine learning algorithms can optimize energy usage, reduce waste, and improve the efficiency of renewable energy systems like wind and solar. In agriculture, AI-driven techniques such as precision farming help monitor crops and manage resources more sustainably.

- **Humanitarian Aid and Disaster Response**: AI systems can analyze satellite imagery and data to predict natural disasters, monitor food shortages, and coordinate disaster response efforts. These technologies are helping global organizations like the United Nations and the World Food Program allocate resources effectively and respond swiftly to crises.

Future Trends and Ethical Considerations

1. The Future of Artificial Intelligence: Innovations on the Horizon

As AI continues to evolve, several cutting-edge trends and developments are poised to shape the future:

- **AI and Quantum Computing**: The next leap in AI may come from quantum computing, which can process vast amounts of data far more quickly than classical computers. Quantum AI has the potential to solve problems that are currently computationally infeasible, revolutionizing fields like drug discovery, cryptography, and materials science.

- **General Artificial Intelligence (AGI)**: While current AI systems are specialized (narrow AI), the long-term goal is to create Artificial General Intelligence (AGI) —machines that possess the ability to perform any intellectual task that a human can. AGI would have self-learning abilities, reasoning skills, and the capacity to make decisions autonomously across a wide range of activities.

- **AI and Human Augmentation**: AI-powered wearable

devices, brain-computer interfaces, and neural implants may one day enhance human capabilities, allowing people to interact with machines directly through thought. This "cyborg" future could extend human intelligence, memory, and physical abilities.

2. Ethical Dilemmas in AI

As AI grows more powerful, it raises significant ethical and societal concerns. Addressing these issues is critical to ensuring that AI benefits humanity as a whole.

- **Bias and Fairness**: One of the major challenges of AI is mitigating bias in decision-making systems. Since AI models are trained on historical data, they can sometimes perpetuate biases related to race, gender, or socioeconomic status. Ensuring fairness in AI systems is a key ethical concern.
- **Job Displacement**: While AI creates new jobs and industries, it also threatens to displace workers in sectors like manufacturing, transportation, and retail. Automation could lead to significant unemployment and societal disruption if not managed thoughtfully.
- **Privacy and Surveillance**: AI systems, particularly in surveillance and data analysis, can pose threats to personal privacy. With facial recognition technology and advanced data-mining techniques, there is a risk of overreach by governments and corporations, leading to a loss of individual freedoms.
- **Autonomous Weapons and Warfare**: The use of AI in military applications, especially autonomous weapons, raises moral questions about accountability, human control, and the potential for unintended conflicts. The development of lethal autonomous weapons systems (LAWS) has prompted debates about international arms control and the future of warfare.

3. Ethical AI for the Future

The future of AI should be guided by responsible development and usage. Policymakers, researchers, and industry leaders are already discussing frameworks for ethical AI that prioritize transparency, accountability, and fairness. International efforts, such as the AI for Good Global Summit organized by the United Nations, aim to harness AI to meet global sustainable development goals while addressing ethical concerns.

Conclusion: AI as a Catalyst for Global Progress

Artificial Intelligence is not just a technological tool—it is a catalyst for societal transformation. From healthcare to education, from industry to global sustainability, AI's influence is rapidly expanding, offering solutions to some of the world's most complex challenges. However, this power comes with immense responsibility. As we move forward into an AI-driven future, it is essential to foster ethical development and empower societies to adapt to the changes AI will bring. Only by doing so can we ensure that AI is a force for positive global progress.

4: BLOCKCHAIN TECHNOLOGY

Historical Background

1. The Early Concepts: Cryptographic Roots

Blockchain technology, though a relatively recent innovation, is deeply rooted in older cryptographic principles. The foundation of blockchain goes back to concepts such as distributed computing, cryptography, and peer-to-peer (P2P) networking, which were explored in various forms long before blockchain was formalized.

- **Early Cryptography**: The first steps toward blockchain came from advancements in cryptography in the 1970s. Public-key cryptography, developed by Whitfield Diffie and Martin Hellman in 1976, was one of the essential building blocks. This cryptographic method allowed secure communication and authentication, a crucial requirement for decentralized systems like blockchain.
- **Digital Cash Concepts**: In the 1980s and 1990s, digital cash systems emerged that foreshadowed blockchain. David Chaum introduced the concept of electronic money, which allowed anonymous digital transactions. Later, cryptographers like Wei Dai and Nick Szabo further developed ideas around decentralized digital currencies and contracts. Szabo's "bit gold" proposal in 1998 is considered a precursor to Bitcoin and blockchain, although it was never implemented.

2. The Emergence of Bitcoin and the Blockchain (2008-2009)

Blockchain technology, as we know it today, was born with the invention of Bitcoin in 2008. This was a turning point in both technological and financial history.

- **Satoshi Nakamoto and the Bitcoin Whitepaper**: In October 2008, an anonymous person or group known as Satoshi Nakamoto published the Bitcoin whitepaper titled "Bitcoin: A Peer-to-Peer Electronic Cash System." This document proposed a decentralized currency that operated without a central authority, using a cryptographically secured distributed ledger—the blockchain. Bitcoin was launched in January 2009, and the first block, known as the "genesis block," was mined by Nakamoto. This marked the birth of blockchain technology.

- **Blockchain: The Technology Behind Bitcoin**: Blockchain served as the underlying technology that made Bitcoin possible. It was designed as a decentralized, immutable ledger that could record all Bitcoin transactions transparently and securely without the need for intermediaries like banks or governments. The blockchain was maintained by a network of nodes, which reached consensus on the validity of transactions through a process known as "proof of work." This consensus mechanism ensured the integrity and security of the ledger.

3. Blockchain Beyond Bitcoin: The Rise of Ethereum (2013-2015)

Although blockchain was initially associated with Bitcoin, developers soon recognized its potential far beyond digital currency. This realization led to the development of Ethereum, a blockchain platform that introduced the concept of smart contracts and decentralized applications (dApps).

- **Vitalik Buterin and the Creation of Ethereum**: In 2013, a young programmer named Vitalik Buterin proposed Ethereum, a new blockchain platform designed to be more versatile than Bitcoin. Buterin's vision was to create a "world computer" where developers could build and run decentralized applications using smart contracts—self-executing contracts with predefined rules. Ethereum's blockchain could handle more than just transactions; it could execute complex programs.

- **The Launch of Ethereum**: In 2015, Ethereum was officially launched, and it quickly gained traction. Developers began creating decentralized applications (dApps) in various industries, including finance, gaming, supply chain management, and more. Ethereum's introduction of smart contracts significantly broadened the scope of blockchain technology and catalyzed the growth of decentralized finance (DeFi) and non-fungible tokens (NFTs).

4. The Evolution of Blockchain: From Hype to Maturity (2016-Present)

By the mid-2010s, blockchain had become a buzzword, attracting attention from businesses, governments, and industries worldwide. However, it also faced challenges in terms of scalability, security, and adoption.

- **Initial Coin Offerings (ICOs) and the Blockchain Boom**: Between 2016 and 2017, blockchain experienced a massive boom, driven by the rise of Initial Coin Offerings (ICOs), a new method of fundraising using cryptocurrencies. Hundreds of blockchain-based projects were launched, and significant capital was raised. While this period saw innovative projects, it also attracted scams and unproven concepts, leading to a subsequent market correction.
- **Scalability Challenges and Solutions**: One of the biggest challenges blockchain faced was scalability—particularly, the ability to process a large number of transactions efficiently. Solutions such as "proof of stake" (PoS) consensus mechanisms, layer-2 scaling solutions (e.g., the Lightning Network), and sharding were introduced to improve the performance of blockchain networks.
- **Blockchain Today**: Today, blockchain is no longer just

about cryptocurrency. It has become a transformative technology with applications across many industries. Its decentralized, secure, and transparent nature makes it suitable for everything from supply chain tracking and digital identity verification to voting systems and decentralized finance.

Global Adoption and Use Cases

1. Blockchain in Finance and Cryptocurrency

The financial industry was the first to experience the disruptive power of blockchain. Cryptocurrencies like Bitcoin, Ethereum, and many others have created a decentralized financial ecosystem that operates outside traditional banking structures.

- **Cryptocurrencies as a Global Asset Class**: Bitcoin, Ethereum, and other cryptocurrencies have become mainstream assets, attracting institutional and retail investors alike. Countries like El Salvador have even adopted Bitcoin as legal tender, while financial giants like Tesla and PayPal have integrated cryptocurrency payments into their platforms. Decentralized finance (DeFi) platforms allow users to lend, borrow, and trade without intermediaries, unlocking new possibilities for financial inclusion, especially in regions with limited banking access.

- **Central Bank Digital Currencies (CBDCs)**: Many governments are exploring blockchain technology to develop Central Bank Digital Currencies (CBDCs). These are digital versions of national currencies that use blockchain for secure transactions. Countries like China, Sweden, and the Bahamas are leading this effort, with China's digital yuan project being one of the most advanced.

2. Blockchain in Supply Chain and Logistics

Blockchain's ability to provide a transparent and immutable ledger has made it ideal for supply chain management. Companies can track products from origin to delivery, ensuring authenticity, safety, and compliance.

- **Global Impact in Trade**: Blockchain is being used to streamline international trade by improving the transparency and efficiency of supply chains. Walmart, IBM, and Maersk have implemented blockchain systems to track the journey of goods, ensuring authenticity and reducing fraud.
- **Food Safety and Traceability**: Blockchain has also found significant use in food safety, where it ensures traceability of products. For example, IBM's Food Trust platform allows retailers and consumers to trace the journey of food products, ensuring their origin, safety, and quality. This system can track produce from farm to table, enhancing food security and reducing waste.

3. Blockchain in Healthcare

In healthcare, blockchain has the potential to transform data management and patient care by providing secure, decentralized records that are accessible by authorized parties while maintaining patient privacy.

- **Health Records and Data Security**: Blockchain technology is being used to secure patient records, giving patients control over their data while allowing healthcare providers to access necessary information securely. For example, Estonia has implemented a blockchain-based health record system for its citizens, making healthcare data easily accessible while ensuring security.
- **Drug Supply Chain and Counterfeit Prevention**: Blockchain is also playing a crucial role in preventing the distribution of counterfeit drugs. Pharmaceutical companies can track the entire lifecycle of a drug, from manufacturing to the end consumer, ensuring the authenticity of products and enhancing patient safety.

4. Blockchain in Digital Identity and Voting

Digital identity is another area where blockchain technology is making a global impact. Blockchain can provide secure, verifiable identities to individuals, especially in regions with weak or non-existent identification systems.

- **Self-Sovereign Identity**: Blockchain enables the concept of self-sovereign identity, where individuals can own and control their personal data, sharing it securely with service providers only when necessary. Countries like India, through initiatives like Aadhaar, and companies like Microsoft, with its decentralized identity platform, are exploring blockchain-based digital identity solutions.
- **Blockchain Voting Systems**: Blockchain has been proposed as a solution for secure and transparent voting systems. Several countries and local governments have experimented with blockchain voting to ensure tamper-proof elections. For instance, West Virginia in the United States piloted blockchain-based voting for overseas military personnel, and Russia explored blockchain voting during its constitutional referendum.

5. Blockchain in Art and Entertainment: NFTs

Non-fungible tokens (NFTs) have brought blockchain into the mainstream art and entertainment industries by allowing the digital ownership of unique assets.

- **The Rise of NFTs**: NFTs, built on blockchain technology, represent ownership of unique digital items such as art, music, and collectibles. Platforms like OpenSea and Rarible allow artists and creators to tokenize their work, creating new revenue streams and giving buyers verifiable ownership of digital assets. NFTs gained global attention when digital artist Beeple sold a piece for $69 million in 2021 at Christie's auction.

- **Tokenizing the Creative Economy**: Beyond digital art, NFTs are being used to tokenize everything from sports memorabilia to virtual real estate. Musicians are exploring NFTs as a way to release exclusive content and offer fans unique experiences. The entertainment industry is likely to see a further proliferation of blockchain-based innovations in the coming years.

Future Outlook: Decentralization and Beyond

1. The Future of Decentralized Finance (DeFi)

DeFi is one of the most significant trends in the blockchain space. With decentralized finance, users can access financial services without intermediaries like banks, using smart contracts to facilitate transactions.

- **DeFi Expansion**: DeFi is poised for rapid growth, as more users and institutions adopt decentralized platforms for lending, borrowing, and trading. The move toward decentralized financial services is expected to disrupt traditional financial systems by providing greater access, transparency, and efficiency.
- **Challenges and Regulation**: While DeFi offers immense potential, it faces challenges, including regulatory uncertainty, security risks, and scalability issues. Governments and regulators worldwide are working to create frameworks to balance innovation with consumer protection, ensuring that DeFi can grow sustainably.

2. Decentralized Autonomous Organizations (DAOs)

The concept of decentralized autonomous organizations (DAOs) is gaining traction as a new form of governance. DAOs are organizations run by code, where decisions are made collectively by token holders through voting mechanisms.

- **New Forms of Governance**: DAOs offer a decentralized

model of governance for businesses, communities, and even nations. They allow for transparent decision-making and minimize the need for centralized leadership. DAOs could redefine how organizations operate in the future, giving power directly to stakeholders.

3. Blockchain and the Internet of Things (IoT)

Blockchain's secure and decentralized nature makes it an ideal partner for the Internet of Things (IoT). As the number of connected devices grows, blockchain can help secure data and automate transactions between devices.

- **Smart Cities and IoT**: In the future, blockchain and IoT could work together to create smart cities, where connected devices manage everything from traffic control to energy distribution. Blockchain would provide a secure and decentralized infrastructure for these systems, ensuring data integrity and preventing cyberattacks.

4. The Role of Blockchain in a Decentralized Web (Web 3.0)

Web 3.0, the decentralized version of the internet, is another area where blockchain will play a critical role. Web 3.0 envisions a world where users have control over their data and online interactions, rather than centralized tech giants.

- **Decentralizing the Web**: Blockchain will be a key infrastructure for Web 3.0, allowing users to own their digital identities, content, and assets. Decentralized platforms and applications will operate on blockchain, providing users with more control over their online presence.

5. Environmental Impact and Sustainability of Blockchain

While blockchain has been criticized for its high energy consumption, particularly in proof-of-work systems like Bitcoin, new developments are focusing on creating more energy-efficient consensus mechanisms.

- **Proof of Stake and Green Blockchain Solutions**: The shift from proof-of-work to proof-of-stake (as seen with Ethereum 2.0) is expected to reduce blockchain's environmental impact significantly. Researchers and developers are also exploring hybrid models and off-chain scaling solutions to improve blockchain's energy efficiency.
- **Blockchain for Environmental Initiatives**: Blockchain can also contribute to sustainability efforts. It can be used to track carbon credits, manage renewable energy distribution, and ensure the transparency of environmental initiatives.

Conclusion

Blockchain technology is transforming industries worldwide, from finance and healthcare to art and governance. Its decentralized, transparent, and secure nature holds immense promise for the future, enabling innovative solutions to longstanding challenges.

As we look toward the future, blockchain's potential seems limitless. From decentralizing finance to creating new models of governance and powering the next generation of the internet, blockchain will continue to play a crucial role in shaping the global technological landscape. However, with this potential comes the need for thoughtful governance, ethical considerations, and continued innovation to ensure that blockchain can fulfill its promise as a force for good in the world.

5: INTERNET OF THINGS (IOT)

Historical Context and Evolution

1. The Origins of IoT: Connecting Machines

The concept of the **Internet of Things (IoT)**, which involves interconnecting everyday devices to the internet to exchange data, has its roots in several technological innovations dating back to the mid-20th century.

- **The First Connected Devices (1960s-1990s)**: The idea of connected machines began as early as the 1960s, when computer networks were first developed. The foundation of modern IoT emerged from **embedded systems**, which integrated processors into devices to manage specific tasks. Over time, innovations in **radio-frequency identification (RFID)**, **wireless communication**, and **sensor technology** enabled objects to communicate with one another and collect data.

- **The Birth of IoT (1999)**: The term "Internet of Things" was first coined in 1999 by **Kevin Ashton**, a British technology pioneer, who was working at Procter & Gamble. Ashton used the term to describe a system where physical objects would be interconnected via the internet using RFID technology. This initial vision was focused on supply chain management but paved the way for broader applications.

- **The Role of Wireless Technologies (2000s)**: With the rise of Wi-Fi, Bluetooth, and mobile networks in the early 2000s, the feasibility of connecting devices to the internet significantly increased. The launch of 3G and 4G mobile networks allowed more devices to communicate in real-time, ushering in the IoT era. These advancements, combined with improvements in cloud computing and **big data analytics**, provided the infrastructure to scale IoT solutions across industries.

2. IoT Takes Shape: From Smart Devices to Smart Systems (2010s)

The 2010s saw the rapid commercialization of IoT technologies as more companies and industries began integrating IoT solutions to optimize processes and improve efficiency.

- **Smartphones and Mobile Applications**: The introduction of the **smartphone** played a pivotal role in the growth of IoT. Devices such as the iPhone, launched in 2007, became central hubs for controlling IoT-enabled devices like **smart thermostats**, **wearables**, and **home automation systems**. Consumers could now use mobile apps to manage everything from their lighting systems to their appliances.
- **Expansion of Industrial IoT (IIoT)**: As IoT matured, its applications spread beyond consumer electronics into industries like **manufacturing**, **energy**, and **logistics**. Referred to as **Industrial IoT (IIoT)**, the technology enabled businesses to monitor equipment performance, manage energy usage, and optimize production lines in real-time.
- **The Rise of Cloud Platforms**: Cloud computing became an essential element in IoT infrastructure. **Amazon Web Services (AWS)**, **Microsoft Azure**, and **Google Cloud** offered platforms that allowed organizations to process and analyze the vast amounts of data generated by IoT devices. These cloud platforms made it easier for companies to scale their IoT applications globally.

3. The Modern IoT Ecosystem (2020s)

Today, IoT is everywhere—from homes and cities to industries and medical facilities. As of 2023, billions of devices are connected to the internet, and the trend is only accelerating.

- **5G Networks and IoT**: The launch of **5G networks** is

further revolutionizing IoT by providing higher speeds, lower latency, and the capacity to connect a massive number of devices simultaneously. This has enabled new applications like **autonomous vehicles**, **smart cities**, and **remote healthcare solutions**.

- **Edge Computing**: A key development in modern IoT is **edge computing**, which processes data closer to where it is generated (at the "edge" of the network), reducing latency and bandwidth usage. This is critical for real-time applications like robotics, machine vision, and autonomous systems.

- **Standardization and Interoperability**: As IoT devices proliferated, the need for standardization and interoperability became essential to ensure that devices from different manufacturers could communicate with each other. Industry groups like the **Internet Engineering Task Force (IETF)** and **International Telecommunication Union (ITU)** are working to create standards that unify the IoT ecosystem.

Global Applications in Various Sectors

1. IoT in Healthcare

The healthcare industry has been one of the early and significant adopters of IoT technologies, with applications that improve patient care, enhance diagnostics, and streamline hospital operations.

- **Remote Patient Monitoring (RPM)**: IoT-enabled devices allow healthcare providers to monitor patients' vital signs remotely. For example, **wearable devices** can track heart rates, blood pressure, and glucose levels, alerting healthcare professionals to abnormalities in real-time. This has been especially useful in managing chronic diseases and reducing hospital visits for patients in rural or underserved areas.

- **Telemedicine**: IoT plays a crucial role in **telemedicine**, where patients can connect with doctors remotely through IoT-based health monitoring systems. During the COVID-19 pandemic, IoT-enabled telemedicine surged as people sought safer ways to access healthcare.
- **Smart Medical Devices**: IoT is also embedded in medical equipment, such as smart insulin pumps, infusion systems, and pacemakers. These devices can transmit real-time data about their performance, enabling timely maintenance and reducing equipment downtime.
- **Hospital Management Systems**: IoT solutions are used to track **hospital assets** like beds, wheelchairs, and medical supplies. Hospitals also use IoT to monitor patient flow, reducing wait times and improving overall efficiency.

2. IoT in Manufacturing and Industry (Industrial IoT or IIoT)

Industrial IoT (IIoT) refers to the application of IoT technology in manufacturing, logistics, and supply chains, which has led to the rise of **Industry 4.0**, a new era of digital manufacturing.

- **Predictive Maintenance**: One of the most prominent use cases for IoT in manufacturing is **predictive maintenance**. IoT sensors are embedded in machinery to monitor performance, detect faults, and predict equipment failures before they occur. This reduces downtime and maintenance costs for manufacturers.
- **Smart Factories**: In smart factories, IoT systems are used to optimize production processes. Machines communicate with each other, sharing data on efficiency and bottlenecks. By integrating IoT with **artificial intelligence (AI)** and **robotics**, manufacturers can achieve greater automation and precision.

- **Supply Chain Optimization**: IoT is used to track goods throughout the supply chain, from production to delivery. IoT devices like RFID tags and GPS trackers provide real-time information on inventory levels, product conditions, and delivery schedules, enabling better logistics management.
- **Worker Safety**: In hazardous industrial environments, IoT wearables help monitor the health and safety of workers. Devices can track vital signs, detect dangerous gas levels, and alert supervisors if a worker is in distress.

3. IoT in Smart Cities and Urban Planning

Cities around the world are embracing IoT to improve public services, optimize energy usage, and enhance citizens' quality of life.

- **Smart Traffic Management**: IoT sensors installed in roads and traffic lights help monitor vehicle flow and adjust traffic signals dynamically to reduce congestion. In cities like Singapore, smart traffic systems use IoT to optimize routes and minimize travel time, while reducing emissions from idling cars.
- **Waste Management**: Smart waste bins equipped with IoT sensors notify waste collection teams when bins are full, optimizing collection routes and reducing waste overflow. Cities like Barcelona have implemented IoT-driven waste management systems to reduce the environmental impact of waste disposal.
- **Energy Efficiency**: Smart meters and grids use IoT to monitor and manage energy consumption in real-time. Cities can track energy usage patterns and adjust energy distribution dynamically, reducing waste and improving sustainability. For instance, **smart streetlights** automatically adjust brightness based on traffic and pedestrian activity, cutting down on energy

usage.

- **Public Safety**: IoT-based **surveillance systems** and **smart emergency response systems** help law enforcement and first responders monitor public spaces, detect potential threats, and respond quickly to emergencies.

4. IoT in Agriculture

In the agricultural sector, IoT is helping farmers improve crop yields, manage resources, and respond to environmental challenges.

- **Precision Agriculture**: IoT devices like **smart sensors** monitor soil conditions, weather patterns, and crop health in real-time, enabling farmers to apply the right amount of water, fertilizer, and pesticides. This reduces waste, lowers costs, and increases crop productivity.
- **Automated Farming**: IoT-based systems control **automated machinery** like irrigation systems, tractors, and drones, which can perform tasks with minimal human intervention. In areas facing labor shortages, this technology is invaluable for maintaining productivity.
- **Livestock Monitoring**: IoT devices are used to track the health and location of livestock. Wearable sensors monitor the vital signs of animals, helping farmers identify sick animals early, improving overall herd health.
- **Supply Chain Transparency**: IoT is also used to track food products throughout the supply chain, from farm to table. This ensures that consumers can trace the origin of their food, improving food safety and sustainability.

5. IoT in Retail

Retailers are using IoT to enhance the shopping experience,

streamline operations, and manage inventory.

- **Smart Shelves**: IoT-enabled smart shelves can automatically detect when products are low in stock and trigger restocking orders, ensuring shelves are always full. This helps retailers manage inventory efficiently and reduce stockouts.
- **Personalized Shopping Experiences**: In-store IoT systems, such as **beacons**, can track customer movements and preferences, allowing retailers to send personalized offers or recommendations to shoppers' smartphones. This enhances customer engagement and increases sales.
- **Supply Chain Management**: Retailers also use IoT to track shipments, monitor product conditions during transit, and ensure timely deliveries. This improves logistics and ensures that products reach consumers in optimal condition.

Future Potential: Smart Ecosystems

The future of IoT is moving toward the creation of **smart ecosystems**, where interconnected devices work together to create seamless, automated environments. These ecosystems are expected to transform various industries and everyday life in significant ways.

1. Smart Homes and Buildings

- **Integrated Smart Systems**: Future smart homes will integrate all devices—appliances, lighting, heating, security systems—into a single, connected ecosystem. Residents will be able to control everything through a unified interface, such as a smartphone app or voice assistant, creating a fully automated living experience.
- **Energy Management**: Smart buildings will optimize energy usage by adjusting temperature, lighting, and energy consumption in real-time, based on occupancy

and external conditions. This will reduce energy waste and lower costs for homeowners and businesses alike.

2. Smart Cities and Urban Ecosystems

- **Connected Infrastructure**: Cities will move toward full IoT integration, where everything from traffic management and waste disposal to public safety and water management is connected. These cities will be able to respond dynamically to changing conditions, improving the quality of life for citizens.

- **Sustainability**: IoT-driven smart cities will focus on sustainability, using data to optimize resource usage, reduce pollution, and enhance environmental protection. **Smart grids**, **renewable energy sources**, and **intelligent waste management** systems will work together to create more sustainable urban environments.

3. Smart Healthcare Ecosystems

- **Personalized Medicine**: IoT will enable more personalized healthcare, where patients can receive tailored treatments based on real-time data from wearable devices and health monitors. AI and IoT will combine to offer predictive healthcare, identifying potential health issues before they become serious.

- **Remote Surgery and Treatment**: With the advancement of 5G, IoT will enable remote surgeries and treatments, where doctors can perform complex procedures on patients located far away, using robotic systems and real-time data feeds.

4. Smart Transportation and Autonomous Vehicles

- **Autonomous Vehicles**: IoT is the backbone of **self-driving cars**, which use sensors, cameras, and real-time data to navigate roads and make decisions without human intervention. As autonomous vehicles become more widespread, IoT will enable them to communicate with each other and with smart infrastructure to improve traffic flow and safety.

- **Smart Transportation Networks**: In the future, entire transportation systems will be interconnected through IoT. Vehicles, buses, trains, and bicycles will communicate with each other and with smart infrastructure to optimize routes, reduce congestion, and ensure efficient public transit systems.

5. Smart Industry and Robotics

- **Industry 5.0**: The future of industrial IoT is moving toward **Industry 5.0**, where human workers and IoT-connected robots work together in collaborative environments. Robots equipped with IoT sensors will assist humans in complex tasks, increasing productivity and efficiency.

- **Hyper-Automation**: IoT will drive the next wave of automation in industries, where machines not only perform tasks but also make decisions and optimize processes autonomously. This hyper-automation will revolutionize manufacturing, logistics, and construction.

Conclusion

The Internet of Things is more than just a collection of connected devices; it represents a fundamental shift in how we live, work, and interact with the world. As IoT continues to evolve, it will create **smart ecosystems** that transform industries, cities, and everyday life.

From **healthcare** and **manufacturing** to **smart cities** and **transportation**, IoT is driving efficiency, innovation, and sustainability. As we look to the future, the development of 5G, edge computing, and AI will unlock even more potential for IoT, making our world smarter, more interconnected, and ultimately, more sustainable.

6: AUGMENTED AND VIRTUAL REALITY

Introduction

Augmented Reality (AR) and Virtual Reality (VR) are rapidly reshaping the way humans interact with the digital and physical worlds. While these technologies have been in development for decades, recent advancements have made them more accessible and impactful across various industries, from gaming and entertainment to healthcare and education. In this chapter, we will explore the **historical development** of AR and VR, examine **global trends and use cases**, and delve into the **future vision** of how these technologies will enhance the human experience.

1. Historical Development

1.1. The Origins of AR and VR

The roots of AR and VR can be traced back to the 1960s, when pioneering work on immersive experiences began.

- **1962**: **Morton Heilig**, an American filmmaker and inventor, developed the **Sensorama**, a mechanical device that combined 3D video, sound, vibrations, and smells to create an immersive experience. This is often considered one of the earliest precursors to VR.
- **1968**: **Ivan Sutherland** and his student **Bob Sproull** created the **Sword of Damocles**, the first head-mounted display (HMD) that offered both VR and AR-like experiences. The device was bulky and required users to be tethered to a ceiling-mounted frame, but it laid the groundwork for future developments.

1.2. The Evolution of Virtual Reality

The term "virtual reality" was coined in the mid-1980s by **Jaron Lanier**, founder of VPL Research. The 1980s and 1990s saw several key advancements:

- **1985-1990**: VPL Research developed a series of VR products, including the **DataGlove**, **EyePhone**, and **DataSuit**, which allowed users to experience immersive, computer-generated environments.
- **1990s**: The video game industry experimented with VR, resulting in products like **Nintendo's Virtual Boy** (1995), though these early devices were limited by technology and failed to gain widespread popularity due to technical limitations and poor user experience.

1.3. The Rise of Augmented Reality

AR gained traction in the early 2000s, but its foundations were set earlier:

- **1992**: **Tom Caudell**, a researcher at Boeing, coined the term **Augmented Reality** to describe technology that superimposed computer-generated information onto real-world environments. Boeing used it for overlaying wiring diagrams onto physical aircraft models.
- **1999**: **NASA** used AR technology in the **X-38 spacecraft**

to project flight paths and real-time data to astronauts, marking one of the first high-profile industrial uses of AR.

1.4. Modern Breakthroughs

The modern era of AR and VR began around the 2010s, thanks to advancements in computer processing, sensors, and display technology.

- **2012**: The release of the **Oculus Rift** Kickstarter campaign brought VR back into the spotlight. Oculus VR, founded by Palmer Luckey, offered a high-quality HMD for an affordable price, revolutionizing the VR space.
- **2013**: **Google Glass**, a wearable AR headset, was introduced by Google. While it faced privacy concerns and market resistance, Google Glass demonstrated the potential for AR in daily life and professional settings.
- **2016**: **Microsoft HoloLens**, a self-contained AR headset, offered an advanced mixed reality experience. HoloLens enabled users to interact with 3D holographic objects in the real world, bridging the gap between AR and VR.

2. Global Trends and Use Cases

2.1. Gaming and Entertainment

Gaming remains the most recognizable use case for AR and VR technologies, with VR offering immersive experiences and AR enhancing real-world environments.

- **VR Gaming**: Oculus Rift, **Sony PlayStation VR**, and **HTC Vive** have revolutionized gaming by allowing players to step inside virtual worlds. These headsets offer 360-degree immersion and create an entirely new level of engagement.
- **AR Gaming**: The mobile game **Pokémon Go** (2016) became one of the most successful AR applications,

blending real-world exploration with AR interactions, and showcasing how AR could be seamlessly integrated into everyday life.

2.2. Healthcare

AR and VR are transforming the healthcare industry by providing new methods for training, diagnostics, and treatment.

- **Medical Training**: VR simulations allow medical students to practice surgeries and other procedures in a risk-free, virtual environment. **AR** helps surgeons by providing real-time data and **3D models** superimposed onto the patient during operations, enhancing precision.
- **Therapy and Rehabilitation**: **VR therapy** has shown promise in treating conditions such as **PTSD**, **anxiety**, and **phobias**, by creating controlled environments in which patients can confront their fears. AR is being used in rehabilitation to guide patients through exercises with real-time feedback.

2.3. Education

AR and VR are becoming key tools in education, providing immersive and interactive learning environments.

- **Virtual Classrooms**: VR enables students to explore historical sites, outer space, or underwater environments without leaving their classrooms. This **experiential learning** enhances engagement and retention of knowledge.
- **AR in Education**: AR apps, like **Google Expeditions**, allow students to visualize complex subjects such as biology and astronomy by overlaying 3D models on their physical environment, making abstract concepts more tangible.

2.4. Retail and E-Commerce

AR and VR are helping reshape the retail experience by allowing customers to visualize products before purchasing.

- **Virtual Showrooms**: With VR, users can step into virtual retail stores from their homes and shop as if they were in a physical location. **IKEA** and other furniture brands have leveraged AR to allow users to "place" furniture in their rooms via smartphone apps, helping them make informed purchasing decisions.

2.5. Architecture and Real Estate

AR and VR are revolutionizing architecture, real estate, and construction by enabling immersive walkthroughs of building designs.

- **Virtual Walkthroughs**: Real estate companies are using VR to allow potential buyers to tour properties remotely. This can significantly cut costs and time, especially for international buyers.
- **AR in Design**: Architects use AR to overlay digital designs on construction sites, making it easier to visualize how a project will look once complete, and helping to detect potential problems early in the design process.

2.6. Military and Defense

The military has been a pioneer in using AR and VR for training and operational purposes.

- **Simulations**: **VR military training** offers soldiers realistic battlefield simulations, where they can practice tactics and decision-making in a safe environment. **AR** is used in real-time battle scenarios to provide soldiers with enhanced situational awareness through smart glasses.

3. Future Vision: Enhancing Human Experience

3.1. Blurring the Lines between Reality and Virtual Worlds

As AR and VR technologies evolve, the distinction between the virtual and physical worlds will continue to blur, resulting in enhanced **immersive experiences** across industries.

- **Mixed Reality (MR)**: The convergence of AR and VR into **mixed reality** will allow users to interact with virtual objects as though they were real, opening new possibilities for **training**, **collaboration**, and **entertainment**.

3.2. Human Augmentation

Future advancements in AR will focus on augmenting human capabilities, offering new ways to enhance performance and interaction with the world.

- **Wearable AR Devices**: As AR headsets become smaller and more integrated into everyday life, users will experience constant real-time information overlays, from language translations to navigation instructions, improving both personal and professional efficiency.

3.3. Social and Collaborative VR

VR is poised to revolutionize social interaction, allowing people to meet in virtual spaces and collaborate as though they were physically present.

- **Virtual Social Spaces**: Platforms like **Facebook Horizon** aim to create virtual social spaces where users can meet, chat, and collaborate in real-time, breaking down the barriers of distance and fostering global collaboration.

3.4. Ethical and Societal Implications

While AR and VR have immense potential, their widespread adoption brings up concerns about privacy, addiction, and ethical issues.

- **Privacy**: The continuous collection of data through AR devices raises questions about surveillance and data security.

- **Addiction**: With VR offering fully immersive experiences, there is concern about **over-immersion**, where users may become too engrossed in virtual worlds, neglecting the physical reality.

3.5. Future Applications in Emerging Fields

AR and VR will continue to find applications in emerging fields like **metaverse development**, **telemedicine**, and **space exploration**. The creation of **digital twins**—virtual replicas of physical objects or environments—will further enhance decision-making, product design, and operational efficiency in industries like manufacturing, transportation, and healthcare.

Conclusion

AR and VR are transforming the way we interact with digital and physical realities. From their early experimental stages to the powerful tools they have become today, these technologies are revolutionizing industries and enhancing human experiences. As we look toward the future, AR and VR will become even more ingrained in everyday life, offering new ways to learn, communicate, and explore both real and virtual worlds. The potential to augment human abilities, create immersive environments, and revolutionize industries will continue to grow, making AR and VR some of the most influential technologies of the 21st century.

7: BIOTECHNOLOGY AND GENETIC ENGINEERING

Introduction

Biotechnology and genetic engineering represent some of the most transformative scientific advancements in human history. By manipulating biological systems and organisms, humanity has achieved remarkable breakthroughs in medicine, agriculture, and industry. These technologies have not only revolutionized our understanding of life but have also led to ethical debates that question the limits of human intervention in natural processes. This chapter traces the **historical progress** of biotechnology from ancient agricultural practices to modern techniques like CRISPR, examines the **global perspective** by highlighting the leading nations and innovations, and discusses the **future innovations** while addressing the ethical implications that come with such advances.

1. Historical Progress: From Agriculture to CRISPR

1.1. Ancient Beginnings: The Agricultural Revolution

The history of biotechnology begins thousands of years ago with the domestication of plants and animals, marking the dawn of agriculture. Early humans practiced selective breeding to cultivate crops and animals with desirable traits, laying the foundation for modern genetic manipulation.

- **Domestication**: As early as 10,000 BC, humans began to domesticate plants like wheat and rice, selecting for traits such as higher yield, better taste, and resistance to environmental conditions. Similarly, animals like cattle, sheep, and dogs were bred for utility, companionship, and food.
- **Fermentation**: Biotechnology in the form of fermentation was used as early as 7,000 BC in ancient

China and the Middle East for producing bread, beer, and wine. This process, involving microorganisms, set the stage for later advances in industrial biotechnology.

1.2. 19th Century: The Foundations of Modern Genetics

The 19th century marked a turning point in biotechnology, as scientific inquiry into the nature of life became more structured.

- **1856–1863**: **Gregor Mendel**, an Austrian monk, conducted experiments on pea plants, laying the foundation for modern genetics. Mendel's laws of inheritance explained how traits are passed from one generation to the next through discrete units known as genes.
- **1869**: **Friedrich Miescher**, a Swiss biochemist, discovered DNA (deoxyribonucleic acid), the molecule that carries genetic information in living organisms. However, the structure and function of DNA remained unknown until much later.

1.3. The Birth of Genetic Engineering:
20th Century Breakthroughs

The 20th century witnessed the birth of modern biotechnology and genetic engineering, particularly with the discovery of the structure of DNA and the development of recombinant DNA technology.

- **1953**: **James Watson** and **Francis Crick**, with contributions from **Rosalind Franklin** and **Maurice Wilkins**, uncovered the double-helix structure of DNA. This discovery revolutionized the field of genetics and opened the door to manipulating genetic material.
- **1973**: The advent of **recombinant DNA technology** by **Herbert Boyer** and **Stanley Cohen** marked the true beginning of genetic engineering. They successfully spliced genes from one organism into another, creating

genetically modified organisms (GMOs). This laid the foundation for gene therapy, biotechnology drugs, and GM crops.

1.4. 21st Century: CRISPR and Gene Editing

The 21st century has seen revolutionary advances in biotechnology, particularly with the development of **CRISPR-Cas9**, a powerful tool for precise genetic editing.

- **2012**: **Jennifer Doudna** and **Emmanuelle Charpentier** published a landmark paper describing how the CRISPR-Cas9 system, originally a bacterial defense mechanism, could be adapted to edit genes in living organisms. CRISPR allows scientists to precisely cut and edit sections of DNA, offering potential cures for genetic diseases, enhancing agricultural productivity, and even altering the genomes of future generations.

2. Global Perspective: Leading Nations and Innovations

2.1. The United States: A Biotechnology Powerhouse

The United States has long been a leader in biotechnology and genetic engineering, driven by both academic research and industry. American companies and research institutions have pioneered numerous innovations.

- **Genetically Modified Crops**: The U.S. is the largest producer of genetically modified (GM) crops. **Monsanto**, now part of Bayer, developed the first genetically engineered crop in the 1990s—herbicide-resistant soybeans—leading to widespread adoption of GM technology in agriculture.
- **Biopharmaceuticals**: U.S. biotechnology companies like **Amgen**, **Genentech**, and **Moderna** have been at the forefront of developing biologic drugs and vaccines. The rapid development of mRNA vaccines, such as those for COVID-19, is one of the most recent successes in biopharma.

2.2. Europe: A Focus on Ethics and Innovation

Europe has a strong tradition of biotechnological research, though its regulatory landscape for genetic engineering is more stringent than that of the U.S.

- **CRISPR in Agriculture**: European countries like the UK, Germany, and the Netherlands are key players in using CRISPR to improve agricultural productivity. However, the European Union (EU) has strict regulations on GM organisms, often prioritizing ethical concerns over commercial adoption.

- **Biomedical Research**: European universities and biotech firms are at the forefront of developing **gene therapies** for rare diseases. Companies like **CRISPR Therapeutics** (Switzerland) and **Oxford Biomedica** (UK) are innovating in the gene-editing space, contributing to advancements in personalized medicine.

2.3. China: Rapid Expansion and Innovation

China has emerged as a major player in biotechnology and genetic engineering, with a government that strongly supports innovation in the life sciences.

- **CRISPR Pioneers**: Chinese scientists were among the first to use CRISPR technology in humans. In 2018, **He Jiankui** controversially claimed to have edited the genes of twin babies, sparking a global debate on the ethics of gene editing in humans. Despite the ethical concerns, China remains at the forefront of CRISPR research, particularly in agriculture and healthcare.

- **Biotechnology Hub**: The Chinese government has invested heavily in biotech startups and research institutions, aiming to make China a global biotechnology hub by 2030. The country is also a leader in **synthetic biology** and **stem cell research**.

2.4. India: Emerging Biotechnology Landscape

India is an emerging player in biotechnology, with a focus on agricultural biotechnology, pharmaceuticals, and bioinformatics.

- **Green Revolution and GM Crops**: India's biotechnology sector gained momentum during the **Green Revolution** of the 1960s and 1970s, which improved crop productivity using advanced agricultural techniques. More recently, India has embraced genetically modified crops like **Bt cotton**, which is resistant to pests and has increased yields for farmers.
- **Pharmaceuticals and Biosimilars**: India is a global leader in **generic drugs** and biosimilars (biologic drugs that are similar to FDA-approved products). Companies like **Biocon** and **Serum Institute of India** are spearheading biotech drug development, including vaccines and cancer therapies.

3. Future Innovations: Ethical Implications and Breakthroughs

3.1. The Promise of Precision Medicine

Biotechnology is driving the development of **precision medicine**, where treatments are tailored to individual patients based on their genetic makeup.

- **Gene Therapy**: CRISPR and other gene-editing technologies are offering hope for curing previously untreatable genetic disorders, such as **cystic fibrosis**, **sickle cell anemia**, and **muscular dystrophy**. These therapies will revolutionize how we approach diseases and enable a more personalized healthcare system.
- **Cancer Immunotherapy**: Advances in biotechnology are helping scientists harness the body's immune system to fight cancer. **CAR-T cell therapy**, where a patient's T-cells are genetically modified to target cancer cells, has already shown success in treating certain types of leukemia.

3.2. Ethical Implications of Genetic Engineering

As the capabilities of genetic engineering advance, so do the ethical concerns surrounding its use.

- **Designer Babies**: CRISPR technology has sparked debates about the possibility of **designer babies**, where parents could potentially select traits like intelligence, appearance, or athletic ability. This raises profound ethical questions about inequality, eugenics, and the moral limits of altering human life.
- **Gene Drives**: Biotechnology allows scientists to engineer **gene drives**, which can spread specific genetic traits through populations at an accelerated rate. While this technology holds potential for eradicating diseases like malaria, it also raises concerns about unintended ecological consequences.

3.3. Future Agricultural Breakthroughs

The future of agriculture will be shaped by biotechnology, with CRISPR and genetic engineering offering solutions to food security, environmental sustainability, and climate change.

- **Climate-Resilient Crops**: Genetic engineering will enable the development of crops that can withstand extreme weather conditions like droughts, floods, and heat, helping to feed the world's growing population in the face of climate change.
- **Sustainable Agriculture**: Biotechnology can reduce the need for harmful pesticides and fertilizers by developing crops with built-in resistance to pests and diseases. This will lead to more sustainable farming practices and reduce the environmental impact of agriculture.

3.4. Synthetic Biology and the Future of Life

The future of biotechnology may also include breakthroughs in **synthetic biology**, where scientists design and construct new biological entities from scratch.

- **Artificial Life**: Synthetic biology could enable the creation of artificial cells and organisms, opening new possibilities for medicine, environmental sustainability, and industry. This could lead to the development of biofuels, biodegradable materials, and even organisms designed to clean up environmental pollution.
- **Biohacking**: The rise of the **biohacker movement** —citizen scientists experimenting with their own biology—presents new ethical challenges and raises questions about the accessibility of biotechnology. As gene-editing tools become cheaper and more available, the potential for unregulated experimentation grows.

Conclusion

Biotechnology and genetic engineering stand at the frontier of human innovation, offering transformative possibilities in medicine, agriculture, and industry. From the historical roots of agriculture and fermentation to the cutting-edge developments of CRISPR, these technologies have reshaped the world in fundamental ways. However, as we look to the future, we must also confront the ethical implications of our growing ability to manipulate life itself. The potential for both great benefit and unintended consequences underscores the need for responsible stewardship of these powerful tools.

8: RENEWABLE ENERGY TECHNOLOGIES

Introduction

The shift towards renewable energy technologies represents one of the most significant transformations in our approach to energy production and consumption. As concerns over climate change, pollution, and fossil fuel depletion grow, the demand for sustainable energy sources has never been more pressing. This chapter explores the **historical context** of energy transitions, examines the **global impact** and leading nations in renewable energy, and discusses **future directions** for innovations aimed at sustainability. Understanding this evolution is vital for young innovators, as the renewable energy sector offers vast opportunities for technological advancements and creative problem-solving.

1. Historical Context of Energy Transition

1.1. The Age of Fossil Fuels

The industrial revolution of the 18th and 19th centuries marked the beginning of the fossil fuel era, with coal, oil, and natural gas becoming the dominant energy sources. This shift enabled unprecedented economic growth and technological advancements but also led to significant environmental degradation.

- **Coal**: Initially, coal was the primary energy source for steam engines and industrial processes. Its abundance fueled rapid industrialization in Europe and North America during the 19th century.
- **Oil and Natural Gas**: The discovery of oil in Pennsylvania in 1859 and subsequent advancements in drilling technology led to the proliferation of oil as a critical energy source for transportation and

industry. Natural gas emerged as a cleaner alternative, increasingly used for heating and electricity generation.

1.2. The Rise of Environmental Awareness

By the mid-20th century, the negative impacts of fossil fuels on the environment became increasingly apparent. The environmental movement gained momentum in the 1960s and 1970s, highlighting issues such as air and water pollution, habitat destruction, and climate change.

- **Silent Spring**: Rachel Carson's 1962 book, *Silent Spring*, raised public awareness about the dangers of pesticides and their impact on the environment, inspiring a broader environmental movement.
- **Oil Crises**: The oil crises of the 1970s underscored the vulnerabilities of relying on fossil fuels, leading to increased interest in alternative energy sources. The 1973 oil embargo prompted many countries to reconsider their energy strategies and invest in research for renewable energy technologies.

1.3. The Advent of Renewable Energy

The late 20th century marked the beginning of a significant shift toward renewable energy sources. Solar, wind, hydroelectric, and geothermal power began to emerge as viable alternatives to fossil fuels.

- **Solar Energy**: The first practical solar cell was developed in the 1950s, but it wasn't until the oil crises that serious investments were made in solar technology. By the 1980s, the first large-scale solar power plants began operation, leading to significant advancements in photovoltaic (PV) technology.
- **Wind Energy**: Wind power also gained traction during this period, with the installation of larger, more efficient turbines. The first modern wind farms were

established in California in the 1980s, paving the way for global wind energy development.

2. Global Impact: Leaders in Renewable Energy

2.1. Europe: Pioneering Renewable Initiatives

Europe has been at the forefront of renewable energy development, driven by ambitious climate goals and strong policy frameworks.

- **Germany**: Germany's *Energiewende* (energy transition) policy aims to transition the country to a sustainable energy system by promoting renewable energy sources, energy efficiency, and grid modernization. Germany is a global leader in solar power and has significantly expanded its wind energy capacity.
- **Denmark**: Denmark is renowned for its wind energy leadership, producing around 47% of its electricity from wind turbines. The country aims to achieve 100% renewable energy by 2050, demonstrating a successful model for integrating renewables into the national grid.

2.2. The United States: Diverse Energy Landscape

The United States has a diverse energy portfolio, with significant investments in both renewable and fossil fuel resources.

- **California**: As a pioneer in renewable energy adoption, California has set ambitious goals for reducing greenhouse gas emissions and increasing the share of renewables in its energy mix. The state aims to reach 100% carbon-free electricity by 2045, with substantial investments in solar and wind power.
- **Texas**: Texas has emerged as the leading state in wind energy production, harnessing its vast land and favorable wind conditions. The state has also seen significant growth in solar energy installations, contributing to its diverse energy landscape.

2.3. China: The Renewable Energy Giant

China has become a global powerhouse in renewable energy, both in terms of production and consumption.

- **Solar Power**: China dominates the global solar PV market, manufacturing over 70% of the world's solar panels. The country has implemented extensive solar farms, aiming for 1,200 GW of installed solar capacity by 2030.
- **Wind Energy**: China is the largest producer of wind energy, with significant investments in onshore and offshore wind farms. The country plans to achieve 1,200 GW of wind power capacity by 2030, further solidifying its leadership in renewables.

2.4. India: Emerging Renewable Energy Leader

India is rapidly expanding its renewable energy capacity, driven by the need for sustainable energy to support its growing population and economy.

- **Solar Energy Initiatives**: India has set ambitious targets for solar energy, aiming to achieve 100 GW of solar power capacity by 2022. The *Jawaharlal Nehru National Solar Mission* has been instrumental in promoting solar energy adoption across the country.
- **Wind Energy Growth**: India is also one of the top wind energy producers globally, with significant installations primarily in states like Tamil Nadu and Gujarat. The government aims to reach 60 GW of wind energy capacity by 2022.

3. Future Directions: Innovations for Sustainability

3.1. Advancements in Solar Technology

The future of solar energy looks promising, with ongoing innovations in photovoltaic technology and energy storage.

- **Perovskite Solar Cells**: Research into perovskite

materials has shown potential for cheaper and more efficient solar cells, possibly exceeding the efficiency limits of traditional silicon cells.
- **Bifacial Solar Panels**: These panels capture sunlight on both sides, increasing energy generation and efficiency. The growing adoption of bifacial technology is expected to enhance the performance of solar installations.

3.2. Wind Energy Innovations

Wind energy technology is also evolving, with advancements in turbine design and energy storage solutions.
- **Larger and More Efficient Turbines**: The trend towards larger turbines with higher capacity factors is expected to lower the cost of wind energy. Innovations in turbine design, such as floating offshore wind farms, open new opportunities for harnessing wind energy in deeper waters.
- **Energy Storage Integration**: Pairing wind energy with advanced battery storage systems can help mitigate the intermittent nature of wind power, ensuring a stable energy supply.

3.3. The Role of Hydrogen

Hydrogen is emerging as a critical player in the future of renewable energy, particularly in decarbonizing sectors that are hard to electrify.
- **Green Hydrogen Production**: Electrolyzing water using renewable electricity to produce hydrogen (green hydrogen) presents a sustainable energy storage solution. This hydrogen can be used as a fuel for transportation, heating, and industrial processes.
- **Hydrogen as an Energy Carrier**: Hydrogen has the potential to serve as an energy carrier, allowing excess renewable energy to be stored and transported to

where it is needed, facilitating the transition to a low-carbon economy.

3.4. Smart Grids and Energy Management

The integration of renewable energy sources into existing energy systems requires innovative grid management solutions.

- **Smart Grids**: The development of smart grids enables better integration of renewables, allowing for real-time monitoring and management of energy resources. Smart grids can optimize energy flow, reduce waste, and enhance the resilience of energy systems.
- **Demand Response Technologies**: These technologies help manage energy consumption by incentivizing users to adjust their usage during peak times, thus balancing supply and demand and enhancing grid stability.

3.5. Policy and Investment for Sustainable Energy

The successful transition to renewable energy requires strong policy frameworks and significant investments.

- **Incentives for Renewables**: Governments must implement supportive policies, such as tax credits, subsidies, and renewable energy mandates, to encourage the adoption of renewable technologies.
- **Investment in R&D**: Continued investment in research and development is crucial for advancing renewable technologies and ensuring their competitiveness in the energy market.

Conclusion

The transition to renewable energy technologies represents a pivotal moment in human history, addressing the pressing challenges of climate change and environmental degradation. From the historical context of fossil fuel reliance to the global leaders in renewable energy, this chapter highlights the urgent need for innovation and sustainability. As young innovators look toward the future, opportunities abound in developing new technologies, advancing policy initiatives, and driving the shift toward a cleaner, greener world. The path to sustainability is filled with challenges, but the potential rewards for society and the planet are immense.

9: ADVANCED ROBOTICS

Introduction

Advanced robotics stands at the intersection of engineering, computer science, and artificial intelligence, revolutionizing how we interact with machines and automate processes. This chapter delves into the **historical development** of robotics, exploring key milestones that have shaped the field. It also examines **global applications** of robotics across various industries, highlighting how robots enhance productivity and efficiency. Finally, we will discuss **future trends**, particularly the rise of collaborative robots (cobots) that work alongside humans, redefining the boundaries of human-machine interaction.

1. Historical Development and Milestones

1.1. Early Concepts and Inventions

The roots of robotics can be traced back to ancient history, where myths and mechanical devices laid the groundwork for modern robotics.

- **Ancient Automata**: Concepts of automated devices can be found in ancient civilizations, such as the Greek engineer Hero of Alexandria, who created steam-powered devices and simple automatons in the first century AD. These early inventions sparked the imagination for what machines could achieve.
- **Leonardo da Vinci's Robot Knight**: In the late 15th century, Leonardo da Vinci designed a mechanical knight that could sit, wave its arms, and move its head. While never built in his lifetime, it showcased the potential of mechanized figures.

1.2. The Industrial Revolution and Mechanization

The Industrial Revolution (18th-19th century) catalyzed the development of machines for manufacturing, laying the foundation for modern robotics.

- **The Jacquard Loom**: Invented in 1804, this loom used punch cards to control the weaving of complex patterns, illustrating early principles of automation that influenced later developments in robotics.
- **The Assembly Line**: Pioneered by Henry Ford in the early 20th century, the assembly line revolutionized manufacturing efficiency and led to the creation of specialized machines designed to automate repetitive tasks.

1.3. The Birth of Modern Robotics

The mid-20th century marked the beginning of modern robotics, driven by advancements in electronics and computer science.

- **George Devol and Unimate**: In the 1950s, George Devol invented the first industrial robot, Unimate, which was later used in General Motors' assembly lines to handle heavy tasks. This milestone marked the entry of robots into industrial settings.
- **Shakey the Robot**: Developed in the 1960s, Shakey was the first robot capable of reasoning about its actions. This project at Stanford Research Institute laid the groundwork for mobile robotics and artificial intelligence.

1.4. Advances in AI and Robotics

The late 20th and early 21st centuries witnessed significant advancements in artificial intelligence and robotics, leading to more sophisticated and capable machines.

- **Robotics and AI Integration**: As computer processing power increased, so did the ability of robots to perform complex tasks. AI algorithms allowed robots to learn from their environments, adapt to changes, and make decisions.
- **Robotic Exoskeletons**: Emerging in the 21st century,

robotic exoskeletons assist individuals with mobility impairments, showcasing the potential for robotics to enhance human capabilities beyond traditional industrial applications.

2. Global Applications Across Industries

2.1. Manufacturing and Automation

Manufacturing remains the most significant sector utilizing robotics, where robots enhance productivity, precision, and safety.

- **Assembly Robots**: Robots are widely used in assembly lines to perform repetitive tasks, such as welding, painting, and material handling. Their ability to work at high speeds and with precision reduces errors and increases output.
- **Collaborative Robots (Cobots)**: Cobots are designed to work alongside human workers, sharing tasks and enhancing productivity. They are increasingly used in small and medium-sized enterprises (SMEs) due to their flexibility and ease of use.

2.2. Healthcare and Medical Robotics

Robotics is transforming healthcare through surgical assistance, rehabilitation, and patient care.

- **Surgical Robots**: Robotic systems like the da Vinci Surgical System enable minimally invasive procedures, allowing surgeons to perform complex operations with precision. These systems enhance patient outcomes and reduce recovery times.
- **Robotic Prosthetics and Exoskeletons**: Advanced robotic prosthetics provide enhanced mobility for amputees, while exoskeletons assist individuals with paralysis in regaining movement, highlighting the potential for robots to improve quality of life.

2.3. Logistics and Supply Chain

The logistics industry has embraced robotics to streamline operations and improve efficiency.

- **Autonomous Mobile Robots (AMRs)**: AMRs navigate warehouses and distribution centers, transporting goods and optimizing inventory management. They reduce labor costs and increase efficiency in supply chain operations.
- **Drones for Delivery**: Unmanned aerial vehicles (drones) are being tested and implemented for package delivery, showcasing the potential for robotics to revolutionize last-mile logistics.

2.4. Agriculture

Robotics is transforming agriculture, enabling precision farming and increased productivity.

- **Agricultural Robots**: Robots are used for planting, harvesting, and monitoring crops. They can operate autonomously or collaboratively with human workers, improving efficiency and reducing labor costs.
- **Drones for Crop Monitoring**: Agricultural drones equipped with sensors provide real-time data on crop health, enabling farmers to make informed decisions about irrigation, fertilization, and pest control.

2.5. Exploration and Robotics in Extreme Environments

Robots are essential for exploration in hazardous or remote environments.

- **Space Exploration**: Rovers like NASA's Perseverance are used to explore Mars, conducting scientific research and gathering data in conditions that are uninhabitable for humans.
- **Underwater Robotics**: Autonomous underwater vehicles (AUVs) are deployed for marine research, oil exploration, and underwater inspections, showcasing robotics' ability to operate in challenging

environments.

3. Future Trends: The Rise of Collaborative Robots

3.1. The Evolution of Collaborative Robotics

As industries evolve, the role of collaborative robots is expected to expand significantly.

- **Enhanced Safety Features**: Future cobots will incorporate advanced safety features, allowing them to work in closer proximity to humans without the need for safety cages. These developments will enable more versatile applications in various settings.
- **User-Friendly Programming**: The emergence of intuitive programming interfaces will allow non-experts to easily program and deploy cobots, making them accessible to a broader range of industries.

3.2. Integration with AI and Machine Learning

The integration of AI and machine learning will continue to enhance the capabilities of robots.

- **Adaptive Learning**: Future robots will leverage machine learning algorithms to adapt to changing environments and tasks. This adaptability will enable them to learn from their experiences, improving their efficiency and effectiveness over time.
- **Human-Robot Interaction**: Advances in natural language processing and computer vision will enable more seamless communication between humans and robots, enhancing collaboration and productivity in the workplace.

3.3. Robotics in Everyday Life

The presence of robotics in everyday life is expected to increase, impacting various sectors.

- **Household Robots**: Domestic robots, such as vacuum cleaners and lawn mowers, will become more advanced, incorporating AI to navigate and perform household tasks autonomously.

- **Service Robots**: Robots in hospitality and retail will assist customers with tasks such as check-in, order taking, and product recommendations, enhancing customer experience and operational efficiency.

3.4. Ethical and Societal Implications

As robotics continues to advance, ethical considerations and societal impacts must be addressed.

- **Job Displacement**: The rise of automation raises concerns about job displacement in certain sectors. Strategies for workforce reskilling and adaptation will be essential to mitigate the impact on employment.
- **Privacy and Security**: As robots collect and process data, concerns about privacy and security will need to be addressed. Developing robust data protection policies will be crucial to maintaining public trust in robotics.

Conclusion

Advanced robotics represents a transformative force across industries, enhancing efficiency, safety, and productivity. From its historical roots to its current applications and future trends, robotics continues to evolve, offering innovative solutions to complex challenges. As young innovators engage with this field, they will have the opportunity to shape the future of robotics, creating technologies that enhance human capabilities and improve the quality of life for people around the world. Embracing the potential of robotics while addressing ethical considerations will be key to ensuring a positive impact on society and the global economy.

10: 3D PRINTING

Introduction

3D printing, or additive manufacturing, has revolutionized the way we design, prototype, and produce a wide variety of objects. This chapter explores the **historical context** of 3D printing technology, tracing its evolution from initial concepts to sophisticated production methods used across industries today. We will examine **global use cases** that highlight the transformative potential of 3D printing, including applications in prototyping, healthcare, aerospace, and more. Finally, we will look at **future possibilities**, focusing on the concept of on-demand manufacturing and its implications for global production and sustainability.

1. Historical Context and Evolution

1.1. Early Concepts of Additive Manufacturing

The roots of 3D printing can be traced back to the 1980s, during a period when digital technologies began to gain traction.

- **Stereolithography (SLA)**: In 1983, Charles Hull invented stereolithography, the first commercial 3D printing technology. This process used ultraviolet light to cure liquid resin into solid layers, enabling the creation of three-dimensional objects from digital models. Hull's innovation laid the foundation for modern 3D printing technologies.
- **Fused Deposition Modeling (FDM)**: In the late 1980s, Scott Crump developed FDM, a process that extrudes thermoplastic filament through a heated nozzle, layer by layer, to create solid objects. This technology would later become the basis for many consumer-grade 3D printers.

1.2. The Growth of 3D Printing Technology

As technology advanced, so did the applications of 3D printing.

- **Patent Expirations and Accessibility**: In the early 2000s, several key patents for 3D printing technologies expired, leading to a surge in innovation and the development of new printing techniques. This democratization of technology facilitated the rise of hobbyist 3D printers, making the technology more accessible to individuals and small businesses.
- **Materials Science Innovations**: The introduction of new materials, such as metals, ceramics, and bio-materials, expanded the range of applications for 3D printing. Advances in materials science have enabled the production of functional parts suitable for various industries, including aerospace, automotive, and healthcare.

1.3. Mainstream Adoption and Industrial Applications

The 2010s marked a pivotal moment in the adoption of 3D printing technology across industries.

- **Industry Recognition**: Major corporations began to recognize the potential of 3D printing for rapid prototyping, customization, and cost-effective production. Companies like General Electric and Boeing started using 3D printing for manufacturing components, significantly reducing lead times and production costs.
- **Inclusion in Design Processes**: 3D printing has been integrated into product design workflows, allowing designers to quickly create and test prototypes. This iterative process accelerates product development and fosters innovation.

2. Global Use Cases: From Prototyping to Production

2.1. Prototyping and Product Development

3D printing is widely used for rapid prototyping, enabling

companies to create physical models of their designs quickly.

- **Speed and Efficiency**: Traditional prototyping methods can take weeks or even months. In contrast, 3D printing allows designers to produce prototypes in a matter of hours, facilitating quicker iterations and refinements.
- **Cost Reduction**: By eliminating the need for expensive molds or tooling, 3D printing reduces the costs associated with prototyping. This accessibility allows startups and small businesses to innovate without significant financial barriers.

2.2. Healthcare Innovations

The healthcare sector has embraced 3D printing for various applications, from creating medical devices to bioprinting tissues.

- **Customized Implants and Prosthetics**: 3D printing enables the production of patient-specific implants and prosthetics, ensuring a better fit and improving patient outcomes. For example, surgeons can create custom hip or knee implants based on a patient's unique anatomy.
- **Bioprinting**: Researchers are exploring bioprinting techniques to create living tissues and organs for transplantation. While still in experimental stages, these advancements hold the potential to address organ shortages and improve regenerative medicine.

2.3. Aerospace and Automotive Industries

The aerospace and automotive industries have adopted 3D printing for manufacturing lightweight, complex parts.

- **Weight Reduction**: In aerospace, reducing weight is critical for fuel efficiency. 3D printing allows for the creation of lightweight components with intricate geometries that would be difficult or impossible to achieve with traditional manufacturing methods.

- **Supply Chain Efficiency**: By enabling localized production, 3D printing can streamline supply chains. Companies can produce parts on demand, reducing inventory costs and lead times.

2.4. Consumer Products and Customization

3D printing is transforming the consumer goods market, allowing for greater customization and personalization.

- **Personalized Products**: Companies are leveraging 3D printing to create customized products, such as jewelry, footwear, and home decor. This trend empowers consumers to design products tailored to their preferences.
- **On-Demand Production**: Rather than maintaining large inventories, businesses can produce items on demand, reducing waste and improving sustainability.

2.5. Construction and Architecture

The construction industry is exploring 3D printing as a method for building structures more efficiently.

- **3D-Printed Homes**: Companies like ICON are pioneering the use of large-scale 3D printers to construct affordable homes. This technology has the potential to address housing shortages and reduce construction costs.
- **Architectural Models**: Architects are using 3D printing to create detailed models of their designs, allowing clients to visualize projects before construction begins.

3. Future Possibilities: On-Demand Manufacturing

3.1. The Concept of On-Demand Manufacturing

On-demand manufacturing represents a paradigm shift in production and supply chain management.

- **Customization at Scale**: As 3D printing technology matures, manufacturers can offer customized products

at scale. This flexibility allows businesses to cater to individual customer preferences without incurring significant costs.
- **Reduced Waste**: Traditional manufacturing often results in excess inventory and material waste. On-demand manufacturing minimizes waste by producing only what is needed, contributing to more sustainable practices.

3.2. Innovations in Materials and Techniques

Future advancements in materials and techniques will further enhance the capabilities of 3D printing.

- **Advanced Materials**: The development of new materials, including bio-compatible materials and high-strength composites, will broaden the range of applications for 3D printing. These innovations will enable the production of parts that meet the demanding requirements of industries such as aerospace and healthcare.
- **Multi-Material Printing**: Future 3D printers will be able to print with multiple materials simultaneously, allowing for more complex designs and functionalities. This capability will lead to the creation of components with integrated features, such as sensors and electronics.

3.3. Integration with Industry 4.0

3D printing will play a crucial role in the advancement of Industry 4.0, characterized by the integration of digital technologies into manufacturing.

- **Smart Manufacturing**: As factories become increasingly connected, 3D printing will be integrated into smart manufacturing systems. Real-time data analysis will optimize production processes, reduce downtime, and improve product quality.

- **Supply Chain Resilience**: On-demand manufacturing enabled by 3D printing can enhance supply chain resilience by allowing companies to produce parts locally, reducing reliance on global supply chains and mitigating risks associated with disruptions.

3.4. Societal and Economic Implications

The widespread adoption of 3D printing and on-demand manufacturing will have significant societal and economic implications.

- **Job Creation and Skills Development**: While automation may displace certain jobs, the growth of 3D printing is likely to create new roles in design, engineering, and manufacturing. As industries evolve, there will be a demand for a workforce skilled in 3D printing technologies.

- **Democratization of Manufacturing**: 3D printing has the potential to democratize manufacturing, allowing small businesses and entrepreneurs to compete with larger corporations. This shift could lead to greater innovation and economic diversity.

Conclusion

3D printing has transformed the landscape of manufacturing, prototyping, and design, offering unprecedented opportunities for innovation and customization. From its historical beginnings to its current applications and future possibilities, 3D printing represents a critical component of the modern manufacturing ecosystem. As young innovators engage with this technology, they have the potential to shape its future, driving advancements that enhance efficiency, sustainability, and creativity across industries. By embracing the possibilities of 3D printing, we can create a future where on-demand manufacturing meets the diverse needs of society while minimizing waste and promoting innovation.

11: SPACE EXPLORATION TECHNOLOGIES

Introduction

Space exploration has captivated humanity's imagination for centuries, representing our innate curiosity about the universe beyond our planet. This chapter delves into the **historical background** of space exploration technologies, tracing key milestones that have defined our journey into space. We will explore the **global contributions and collaborations** that have propelled us into the cosmos, showcasing the efforts of various nations and organizations. Finally, we will examine the **future outlook** for space exploration, focusing on the rise of commercial space travel and the potential for human exploration beyond Earth.

1. Historical Background: Key Milestones in Space Travel

1.1. The Dawn of Space Exploration

The exploration of space began as a dream and gradually transformed into a reality through scientific advancements and technological innovations.

- **Early Theories and Concepts**: The idea of space travel dates back to ancient civilizations. Philosophers like Johannes Kepler and Isaac Newton laid the groundwork for understanding the mechanics of celestial bodies. In the 19th century, visionaries like Jules Verne penned science fiction works that inspired generations to think beyond Earth.
- **The First Artificial Satellite**: On October 4, 1957, the Soviet Union launched **Sputnik 1**, the first artificial satellite, marking a significant milestone in space exploration. This event ignited the space race between

the United States and the Soviet Union, prompting both nations to accelerate their space programs.

1.2. The Space Race

The 1960s were marked by intense competition between the two superpowers as they vied for supremacy in space.

- **Human Spaceflight**: In 1961, Soviet cosmonaut Yuri Gagarin became the first human to travel into space aboard **Vostok 1**, completing an orbit around Earth. This achievement showcased the Soviet Union's technological prowess and spurred the U.S. to intensify its efforts in space exploration.
- **Apollo Program**: In 1969, NASA successfully landed astronauts Neil Armstrong and Buzz Aldrin on the Moon during the **Apollo 11** mission. This monumental achievement not only represented a significant scientific and technological accomplishment but also a triumph in the space race.

1.3. Expanding Horizons

Following the initial breakthroughs, space exploration entered a new phase characterized by collaborative international efforts and advancements in technology.

- **Space Shuttle Era**: NASA's Space Shuttle program, which began in 1981, facilitated regular human access to space. The reusable shuttle design allowed for missions ranging from satellite deployment to scientific research and construction of the International Space Station (ISS).
- **International Space Station**: The ISS, launched in 1998, symbolizes international collaboration in space exploration. It serves as a research laboratory and living space for astronauts from around the world, demonstrating the potential for peaceful cooperation in space endeavors.

2. Global Contributions and Collaborations

2.1. International Partnerships

Space exploration is increasingly becoming a collaborative effort among nations, with various countries contributing to advancements in technology and research.

- **European Space Agency (ESA)**: Established in 1975, ESA comprises 22 member states that collaborate on space missions, satellite development, and scientific research. ESA has played a pivotal role in Earth observation, planetary exploration, and human spaceflight initiatives.
- **Russian Space Agency (Roscosmos)**: Building on the legacy of the Soviet space program, Roscosmos continues to contribute to space exploration through crewed missions, satellite launches, and participation in the ISS.
- **Indian Space Research Organisation (ISRO)**: India has emerged as a significant player in space exploration. With missions like the **Chandrayaan** lunar exploration program and the **Mars Orbiter Mission**, ISRO has gained international recognition for its cost-effective and successful space endeavors.

2.2. Commercial Partnerships

The rise of commercial space companies has transformed the landscape of space exploration, leading to innovative collaborations between the public and private sectors.

- **SpaceX**: Founded by Elon Musk, SpaceX has revolutionized space travel through the development of reusable rocket technology. The company has successfully launched crewed missions to the ISS and aims to facilitate Mars colonization through the **Starship** program.
- **Blue Origin**: Founded by Jeff Bezos, Blue Origin

focuses on suborbital space tourism and orbital missions. The company's **New Shepard** rocket has successfully conducted crewed flights, paving the way for commercial space tourism.

- **Collaboration with NASA**: NASA has engaged in partnerships with commercial companies to further its exploration goals. The **Commercial Crew Program** enables private companies to transport astronauts to the ISS, enhancing access to low Earth orbit.

3. Future Outlook: Commercial Space Travel and Exploration

3.1. The Emergence of Commercial Space Travel

The future of space exploration is poised to witness a significant shift toward commercial activities, democratizing access to space for individuals and organizations.

- **Space Tourism**: Companies like SpaceX, Blue Origin, and Virgin Galactic are developing programs for space tourism, allowing civilians to experience space travel. This burgeoning industry is expected to grow, with potential flights to suborbital altitudes and eventually orbital experiences.
- **Infrastructure Development**: As commercial space travel becomes more prevalent, the development of space infrastructure, including spaceports and habitats, will be crucial for supporting tourism and exploration efforts.

3.2. Human Exploration of Mars

Mars exploration is a primary goal for space agencies and private companies, with plans to send humans to the Red Planet within the next few decades.

- **NASA's Artemis Program**: NASA's Artemis program aims to return humans to the Moon by the mid-2020s, serving as a stepping stone for future Mars missions. The experience gained from lunar exploration will

inform the technologies and strategies needed for crewed missions to Mars.
- **SpaceX's Starship**: SpaceX envisions sending the first humans to Mars aboard its Starship vehicle. With ambitious timelines, SpaceX aims to establish a sustainable human presence on Mars, focusing on colonization and resource utilization.

3.3. Advanced Technologies for Exploration

The future of space exploration will be driven by advancements in technology, enabling more ambitious missions and scientific discoveries.

- **Artificial Intelligence and Robotics**: AI and robotics will play crucial roles in future space missions, enhancing autonomous navigation, data analysis, and decision-making. Robotic explorers and drones will be essential for surveying distant planets and moons before human arrival.
- **In-Situ Resource Utilization (ISRU)**: Future missions will prioritize ISRU technologies, enabling astronauts to utilize local resources for sustenance, fuel, and construction. This approach will be critical for sustaining long-duration missions on Mars and beyond.

3.4. Ethical Considerations and Sustainability

As space exploration expands, ethical considerations surrounding resource utilization and the preservation of celestial bodies will become increasingly important.

- **Space Debris**: The growing concern of space debris poses risks to satellites and space missions. Future strategies will need to address debris mitigation and removal to ensure the long-term sustainability of space activities.
- **Planetary Protection**: Ensuring that missions do not

contaminate other celestial bodies is essential for preserving the integrity of scientific research. Ethical guidelines will need to be established to govern planetary exploration and the potential for life beyond Earth.

Conclusion

Space exploration technologies have evolved significantly, from the early days of human spaceflight to the current landscape characterized by international collaboration and commercial endeavors. The future promises exciting possibilities, including commercial space travel, Mars exploration, and advancements in technology that will redefine our understanding of the universe. As we look to the stars, the potential for discovery and innovation remains boundless, inviting the next generation of explorers to dream big and push the boundaries of what is possible. Through collaboration, ethical considerations, and technological advancements, humanity is poised to embark on a new era of exploration, unlocking the mysteries of the cosmos and expanding our presence beyond Earth.

12: CYBERSECURITY INNOVATIONS

Introduction

As the digital landscape evolves, so do the threats that accompany it. Cybersecurity has emerged as a critical field in protecting sensitive data, infrastructure, and national security. This chapter will provide a comprehensive overview of **cybersecurity innovations**, tracing the **historical context** of cybersecurity development, exploring **global perspectives on cyber threats**, and examining **future trends**, particularly the role of artificial intelligence (AI) in enhancing cyber defense mechanisms.

1. Historical Context of Cybersecurity Development

1.1. Early Developments in Cybersecurity

The roots of cybersecurity can be traced back to the dawn of computing and networking, where the first significant threats were primarily accidental or caused by human error.

- **The Birth of Computer Security (1970s)**: The concept of computer security began to take shape with the development of ARPANET, the precursor to the modern Internet. Early security measures focused on physical access control to mainframe computers. In 1971, Ray Tomlinson introduced email, inadvertently creating new vulnerabilities and paving the way for future exploits.

- **First Computer Virus (1986)**: The **Brain virus**, created by two Pakistani brothers, marked the first known computer virus to spread beyond a single computer. This event highlighted the need for protective measures against malicious software, leading to the development of antivirus programs.

1.2. The Evolution of Cybersecurity

As the Internet became more accessible in the 1990s, the

cybersecurity landscape evolved rapidly, with new threats emerging alongside advancements in technology.

- **The Rise of Cybercrime (1990s)**: With the advent of the World Wide Web, cybercrime began to flourish. Hackers exploited vulnerabilities in systems, leading to significant financial losses and breaches of privacy. Notable incidents included the **Mafiaboy** hack in 2000, which took down several major websites, including CNN and eBay.

- **Formation of Cybersecurity Standards**: In response to the growing threats, organizations began to develop cybersecurity frameworks and standards. The **ISO/IEC 27001** standard, established in 2005, provided guidelines for establishing, implementing, maintaining, and continuously improving information security management systems.

1.3. Modern Cybersecurity Frameworks

The 21st century has witnessed an explosion of cybersecurity innovations, spurred by the proliferation of connected devices and the increasing sophistication of cyber threats.

- **Public-Private Partnerships**: Governments and private organizations have recognized the need for collaboration in combating cyber threats. Initiatives such as the **U.S. Department of Homeland Security's** Cybersecurity Strategy emphasize the importance of information sharing and coordination among stakeholders.

- **Advanced Security Protocols**: The implementation of advanced security protocols, such as **Transport Layer Security (TLS)** and **Secure Socket Layer (SSL)**, has become standard practice to protect data in transit. Additionally, multi-factor authentication (MFA) and encryption technologies have bolstered security measures across platforms.

2. Global Perspectives on Cyber Threats

2.1. The Landscape of Cyber Threats

Cyber threats have evolved into a global issue, affecting individuals, businesses, and governments. Understanding the nature of these threats is essential for effective cybersecurity.

- **Types of Cyber Threats**:
    - **Malware**: Malicious software, including viruses, worms, and ransomware, can compromise systems and data. Ransomware attacks, in particular, have gained notoriety, demanding payment for the decryption of stolen data.
    - **Phishing**: Cybercriminals use deceptive emails and websites to trick individuals into revealing sensitive information, such as passwords and credit card numbers.
    - **Distributed Denial of Service (DDoS) Attacks**: Attackers overload systems with traffic, rendering services unavailable. High-profile DDoS attacks have targeted major companies and government agencies, causing significant disruption.

2.2. Global Cybersecurity Initiatives

In response to the increasing prevalence of cyber threats, nations and international organizations have implemented strategies to enhance cybersecurity resilience.

- **United Nations (UN)**: The UN has emphasized the importance of cybersecurity as a global issue, promoting international cooperation to combat cybercrime. Initiatives like the **UN Office on Drugs and Crime (UNODC)** focus on building capacity and sharing best practices among nations.
- **European Union (EU)**: The EU established the

General Data Protection Regulation (GDPR) in 2018, setting stringent guidelines for data protection and privacy. The regulation aims to enhance user control over personal data and impose penalties for non-compliance.

- **National Cybersecurity Strategies**: Countries worldwide have developed comprehensive cybersecurity strategies. For instance, the **U.S. National Cyber Strategy** emphasizes securing critical infrastructure, protecting privacy, and fostering innovation in cybersecurity technologies.

3. Future Trends: The Role of AI in Cyber Defense

3.1. The Emergence of AI in Cybersecurity

Artificial intelligence is poised to revolutionize cybersecurity, enabling organizations to respond to threats more effectively and proactively.

- **Threat Detection and Response**: AI-driven systems can analyze vast amounts of data to identify patterns indicative of cyber threats. Machine learning algorithms enhance threat detection capabilities, allowing organizations to respond to incidents in real-time.
- **Automated Incident Response**: AI can automate incident response processes, reducing the time it takes to mitigate threats. Automated systems can isolate affected devices, block malicious traffic, and initiate predefined response protocols, minimizing damage.

3.2. Predictive Analytics and Threat Intelligence

AI enhances predictive analytics, allowing organizations to anticipate potential threats based on historical data and behavioral patterns.

- **Behavioral Analysis**: AI systems can monitor user behavior to identify anomalies that may indicate a

security breach. By establishing baselines for normal behavior, organizations can detect deviations that warrant investigation.
- **Threat Intelligence Sharing**: AI can facilitate the sharing of threat intelligence across organizations, enabling a collaborative approach to cybersecurity. By aggregating and analyzing data from various sources, AI can provide insights into emerging threats and vulnerabilities.

3.3. Ethical Considerations and Challenges

While AI offers significant benefits for cybersecurity, it also raises ethical considerations and challenges that must be addressed.
- **Bias and Discrimination**: AI algorithms can inadvertently incorporate biases present in the data they are trained on, leading to discriminatory practices in threat detection. Ensuring fairness and accountability in AI systems is essential for building trust.
- **Adversarial AI**: Cybercriminals may leverage AI to develop sophisticated attack strategies, creating a cat-and-mouse game between attackers and defenders. Organizations must stay ahead of evolving tactics to protect against AI-driven threats.

3.4. The Future of Cybersecurity Innovation

The integration of AI into cybersecurity is only the beginning. The future of cybersecurity will be characterized by ongoing innovations and collaborations.
- **Zero Trust Architecture**: The Zero Trust model advocates for verifying every access request, regardless of location. As organizations adopt this approach, AI will play a crucial role in continuously assessing user behavior and access rights.
- **Quantum Computing**: The advent of quantum

computing poses new challenges and opportunities for cybersecurity. While quantum computing may enhance encryption methods, it also raises concerns about the potential to break existing cryptographic protocols.

- **Human-Centric Security**: The future of cybersecurity will emphasize human involvement, recognizing that employees play a critical role in maintaining security. AI can assist in training and educating individuals to recognize threats and adopt best practices.

Conclusion

Cybersecurity innovations have come a long way from their humble beginnings, evolving in response to the increasingly complex digital landscape. As cyber threats continue to pose significant challenges, the integration of artificial intelligence into cybersecurity practices promises to enhance threat detection, response, and overall resilience. However, ethical considerations and challenges must be addressed to ensure that AI is used responsibly and effectively. As we look to the future, the need for collaboration among nations, organizations, and individuals is paramount in safeguarding our digital world and fostering a secure environment for all. Through ongoing innovation and proactive measures, we can build a robust cybersecurity framework that protects against the evolving threats of tomorrow.

13: FUTURE TECHNOLOGIES AND TRENDS

Introduction

As we stand on the brink of the next technological revolution, emerging technologies promise to redefine our societies, economies, and interactions with the world. This chapter will explore the landscape of future technologies, including **quantum computing** and **climate engineering**, provide a global context for the international race for innovation, and discuss the potential implications these advancements may have on society and ethical considerations that arise from them.

1. Overview of Emerging Technologies

1.1. Quantum Computing

Quantum computing represents a monumental leap in computational capability, harnessing the principles of quantum mechanics to process information in fundamentally new ways.

- **Principles of Quantum Computing**: Unlike classical computers, which use bits (0s and 1s) to process data, quantum computers use **qubits**. A qubit can exist in multiple states simultaneously, allowing quantum computers to perform many calculations at once, dramatically increasing their processing power for certain tasks.
- **Potential Applications**:
  - **Cryptography**: Quantum computers could break traditional encryption methods, necessitating the development of quantum-resistant algorithms.
  - **Drug Discovery**: By simulating molecular interactions at a quantum level, researchers can identify potential new drugs more

efficiently.
- **Optimization Problems**: Industries such as logistics and finance can benefit from quantum computing's ability to solve complex optimization problems quickly.

1.2. Climate Engineering

Climate engineering, or geoengineering, refers to deliberate interventions in the Earth's climate system to mitigate the effects of climate change.

- **Types of Climate Engineering**:
    - **Solar Radiation Management (SRM)**: Techniques such as stratospheric aerosol injection aim to reflect a small percentage of the sun's light back into space, potentially cooling the planet.
    - **Carbon Dioxide Removal (CDR)**: Methods like direct air capture and ocean fertilization seek to remove CO2 from the atmosphere and sequester it, helping to reduce greenhouse gas concentrations.
- **Challenges and Controversies**: Climate engineering raises ethical and governance questions, including potential side effects, moral hazards, and the risk of unequal impacts across different regions.

1.3. Other Emerging Technologies

In addition to quantum computing and climate engineering, several other technologies are on the horizon:

- **Biotechnology and Genetic Engineering**: Advances in CRISPR and synthetic biology promise to revolutionize medicine, agriculture, and environmental conservation.
- **5G and Beyond**: The rollout of 5G technology will enable faster communication and the proliferation

of smart devices, enhancing IoT applications and connectivity.
- **Neurotechnology**: Developments in brain-computer interfaces aim to connect human brains directly with computers, potentially transforming healthcare and human capabilities.

2. Global Context: International Race for Innovation

2.1. The Global Landscape of Innovation

The race for technological supremacy is not confined to any single nation; it is a global phenomenon with significant geopolitical implications.

- **National Strategies for Innovation**: Countries worldwide are developing strategies to boost their technological capabilities. For example, the **U.S. National Quantum Initiative Act** promotes research and development in quantum technology, while China aims to lead in artificial intelligence and quantum computing by investing heavily in research and talent.
- **International Collaborations**: Collaborative efforts, such as the **European Union's Horizon Europe program**, foster cross-border research and innovation, emphasizing the importance of working together to tackle global challenges.

2.2. The Role of Corporations and Startups

Private enterprises play a crucial role in the innovation landscape, driving advancements and competing on a global scale.

- **Corporate Investment in R&D**: Tech giants like Google, Amazon, and Microsoft invest billions in research and development to stay ahead of the curve in emerging technologies. Their initiatives shape the direction of technological advancement and set the pace for the industry.
- **Startup Ecosystem**: Startups are often at the forefront

of innovation, bringing fresh ideas and agility to the market. They contribute significantly to sectors such as biotechnology, renewable energy, and artificial intelligence, often working in tandem with established corporations.

2.3. Ethical and Regulatory Considerations

As nations race to innovate, ethical and regulatory frameworks must evolve to address the implications of emerging technologies.

- **Establishing Guidelines**: Governments and international bodies are tasked with creating guidelines that ensure responsible development and deployment of technologies. For instance, discussions surrounding the ethical use of AI and biotechnology are gaining prominence.
- **Balancing Innovation and Safety**: Striking a balance between fostering innovation and ensuring public safety is essential. Regulatory bodies must adapt to the rapid pace of technological advancement while addressing public concerns and potential risks.

3. Future Implications for Society and Ethics

3.1. Societal Transformations

The integration of emerging technologies into daily life will bring profound changes to society.

- **Workforce Displacement**: Automation and AI have the potential to displace jobs across various sectors. While some jobs will become obsolete, new roles will emerge, necessitating a shift in workforce skills and training.
- **Access and Inequality**: The benefits of emerging technologies may not be equally distributed, leading to a widening gap between those with access to advanced technologies and those without. Ensuring equitable access will be critical in mitigating disparities.
- **Changing Social Dynamics**: Technologies like virtual

reality and social media continue to reshape how we interact, communicate, and form communities. The implications for mental health, privacy, and societal norms will require careful consideration.

3.2. Ethical Dilemmas and Considerations

The rapid pace of technological advancement raises ethical questions that must be addressed to ensure responsible innovation.

- **Privacy and Surveillance**: As technologies like AI and IoT collect vast amounts of data, concerns over privacy and surveillance become increasingly relevant. Balancing security needs with individual rights is crucial.
- **Moral Implications of Climate Engineering**: Interventions in the climate system raise moral questions about humanity's role in nature and the potential unintended consequences of geoengineering.
- **AI Ethics**: The development of AI technologies must prioritize ethical considerations, including transparency, accountability, and bias mitigation. Establishing ethical guidelines for AI deployment is essential to foster trust and acceptance.

3.3. Preparing for the Future

To harness the potential of emerging technologies while mitigating risks, a proactive approach is necessary.

- **Education and Workforce Development**: Investing in education and training will be vital to equip future generations with the skills needed to thrive in a rapidly changing technological landscape.
- **Encouraging Innovation with Responsibility**: Policymakers must foster an environment that encourages innovation while holding companies accountable for the societal implications of their

technologies.
- **Global Cooperation**: Addressing the challenges posed by emerging technologies will require international collaboration. By working together, nations can develop shared standards, best practices, and policies to ensure a safer and more equitable technological future.

Conclusion

The future of technology promises a transformative impact on society, economy, and culture. Emerging technologies such as quantum computing and climate engineering hold immense potential for addressing global challenges and enhancing human capabilities. However, as we navigate this new frontier, it is essential to consider the ethical implications, societal transformations, and the importance of equitable access to these advancements. By fostering a culture of responsible innovation and global cooperation, we can harness the benefits of future technologies while ensuring a sustainable and just society for all. The choices we make today will shape the technological landscape of tomorrow, underscoring the need for thoughtful action and collaboration in an increasingly interconnected world.

14: FOSTERING INNOVATION AND ENTREPRENEURSHIP

Introduction

In an era characterized by rapid technological advancement and global connectivity, fostering innovation and entrepreneurship has never been more critical. This chapter will explore strategies to encourage young innovators, provide inspiring case studies of successful entrepreneurs, and highlight resources available for personal and professional development. By equipping the next generation with the tools, mindset, and support they need, we can cultivate a thriving culture of innovation that drives economic growth and societal progress.

1. Encouraging Young Innovators: Tips and Strategies

1.1. Cultivating an Innovative Mindset

Encouraging young innovators starts with fostering the right mindset. Here are some strategies to nurture creativity and innovation:

- **Promote Curiosity**: Encourage young people to ask questions, explore their interests, and seek answers. Curiosity drives innovation by prompting individuals to look beyond the obvious and discover new solutions.

- **Embrace Failure**: Teach young innovators that failure is a part of the creative process. Sharing stories of famous entrepreneurs who faced setbacks before achieving success can help normalize failure and encourage resilience.

- **Encourage Critical Thinking**: Foster analytical skills through problem-solving exercises. Engaging students in discussions about real-world challenges and inviting them to propose innovative solutions can stimulate critical thinking.

1.2. Providing Practical Experiences

Hands-on experiences can be instrumental in developing innovative skills. Consider the following approaches:

- **Workshops and Hackathons**: Organizing workshops and hackathons allows young innovators to collaborate, brainstorm, and prototype their ideas in a supportive environment. These events can encourage teamwork, creativity, and rapid iteration.
- **Mentorship Programs**: Pairing young innovators with experienced mentors can provide guidance, feedback, and valuable networking opportunities. Mentorship fosters personal growth and helps innovators navigate the challenges of entrepreneurship.
- **Internships and Apprenticeships**: Real-world experience in startups or innovative companies can give young people insight into the entrepreneurial process. Internships can expose them to industry practices, networking, and skill development.

1.3. Building Supportive Communities

Creating an ecosystem that supports innovation is essential. Strategies include:

- **Networking Events**: Organizing networking events, meetups, and speaker sessions can connect aspiring innovators with industry professionals, potential investors, and fellow entrepreneurs.
- **Innovation Hubs and Incubators**: Establishing local innovation hubs or incubators provides young entrepreneurs with access to resources, mentorship, and collaboration opportunities. These spaces can foster creativity and entrepreneurship.
- **Online Platforms**: Utilize social media and online forums to create communities where young innovators can share ideas, seek feedback, and collaborate on

projects.

2. Case Studies of Successful Entrepreneurs

2.1. Ritesh Agarwal – OYO Rooms

Ritesh Agarwal founded OYO Rooms at the age of 19. He identified a gap in the budget accommodation sector in India and leveraged technology to address it. Through relentless dedication, Ritesh expanded OYO into one of the largest hotel chains globally, revolutionizing the hospitality industry.

- **Key Takeaways**:
  - **Identifying Gaps**: Ritesh's success demonstrates the importance of recognizing unmet needs in the market.
  - **Scalability**: OYO's business model is based on scalability, allowing rapid growth through partnerships with hotels.

2.2. Kiran Mazumdar-Shaw – Biocon

Kiran Mazumdar-Shaw founded Biocon, a biopharmaceutical company, after realizing the potential of biotechnology in healthcare. Starting in her garage, Kiran's vision led Biocon to become a leader in the global biopharmaceutical market.

- **Key Takeaways**:
  - **Persistence**: Kiran faced numerous challenges but remained committed to her vision.
  - **Innovation in Healthcare**: Her focus on affordable healthcare solutions highlights the role of innovation in addressing societal issues.

2.3. N. R. Narayana Murthy – Infosys

N. R. Narayana Murthy co-founded Infosys, an IT services company, in 1981. He was instrumental in establishing the company as a global leader in IT consulting and services.

- **Key Takeaways**:

- **Leadership and Values**: Murthy emphasized corporate governance, ethics, and employee welfare, setting a strong foundation for Infosys's culture.
- **Global Vision**: His foresight in the IT industry positioned Infosys as a frontrunner in the tech revolution.

3. Resources for Development: Organizations and Online Courses

3.1. Organizations Supporting Innovation and Entrepreneurship

Several organizations focus on nurturing young entrepreneurs through mentorship, funding, and training:

- **TiE (The Indus Entrepreneurs)**: A global network that supports entrepreneurs through mentorship, networking opportunities, and access to funding.
- **NASSCOM (National Association of Software and Service Companies)**: Provides resources and support for startups in the technology sector, including training programs, networking events, and access to funding.
- **Startup India**: An initiative by the Government of India that provides various support systems, including funding, incubation, and policy support for startups.

3.2. Online Courses and Learning Platforms

Numerous online platforms offer courses designed to develop entrepreneurial skills and foster innovation:

- **Coursera**: Offers courses from top universities on entrepreneurship, business strategy, and innovation management.
- **edX**: Provides access to courses on entrepreneurship, startup development, and innovation from prestigious

institutions worldwide.
- **Udacity**: Focuses on tech skills and offers nanodegrees in areas like AI, data science, and programming, which are crucial for aspiring innovators in the tech industry.
- **Khan Academy**: Provides free educational resources on entrepreneurship, finance, and business fundamentals.

Conclusion

Fostering innovation and entrepreneurship is vital for creating a vibrant economy and addressing global challenges. By encouraging young innovators through practical experiences, supportive communities, and access to resources, we can empower the next generation to turn their ideas into reality. The case studies of successful entrepreneurs serve as inspiration, illustrating the transformative power of innovation and the importance of perseverance. As we invest in the development of young innovators, we lay the groundwork for a future rich in creativity, technological advancement, and societal progress.

15: CONCLUSION

1. Recap of Key Themes and Insights

As we reach the end of this exploration into the world of cutting-edge technologies, it is essential to reflect on the key themes and insights discussed throughout the book. Each chapter has highlighted how technology serves as a catalyst for change, shaping societies and transforming industries across the globe.

- **Historical Context and Evolution**: Understanding the historical context of technology—from the invention of the wheel to the rise of artificial intelligence—has revealed the gradual but profound impact of human ingenuity. Technological evolution is not merely about innovation but also about adaptation, resilience, and the pursuit of knowledge.

- **Global Impact and Collaboration**: The book underscored the significance of global contributions to technological advancements. Countries around the world have played pivotal roles in shaping these technologies, emphasizing the collaborative nature of innovation. By sharing ideas, resources, and expertise, nations can collectively address challenges and drive progress.

- **Future Outlook and Ethical Considerations**: Each technology discussed also brought forth the need for a thoughtful approach to the future. With advancements like AI, biotechnology, and renewable energy, ethical considerations are paramount. As we leverage technology to solve problems, we must also consider the implications of our innovations on society, privacy, and the environment.

- **Fostering Innovation**: Encouraging a culture of innovation and entrepreneurship among young people emerged as a crucial theme. By nurturing creativity, resilience, and a willingness to take risks, we can empower the next generation to tackle the challenges of tomorrow. The success stories of entrepreneurs demonstrate that with the right mindset and support, individuals can make a significant impact.

2. Call to Action: Engaging with Technology for a Better Future

As we conclude this journey through the transformative power of technology, we extend a call to action to readers—particularly young innovators, students, and aspiring entrepreneurs:

- **Stay Curious and Open-Minded**: Embrace a mindset of curiosity and lifelong learning. The world of technology is ever-evolving, and maintaining an open mind allows you to adapt and thrive in a dynamic landscape. Explore new ideas, ask questions, and seek to understand how technology can be used to address real-world problems.
- **Engage with Your Community**: Participate in local innovation hubs, workshops, and networking events. Engaging with like-minded individuals can spark new ideas and collaborations. Seek mentorship from experienced professionals who can guide you on your journey.
- **Be Ethical Innovators**: As you explore the potential of technology, remember the ethical implications that accompany innovation. Consider how your ideas can contribute to a better society and environment. Strive for solutions that enhance quality of life while respecting the rights and well-being of all individuals.
- **Pursue Education and Skills Development**: Take advantage of online courses, workshops, and resources available for skill development. Equip yourself with the knowledge and tools needed to turn your ideas into

reality. Whether it's programming, design thinking, or business management, investing in your education will pay dividends in the future.

- **Dream Big and Take Action**: Don't be afraid to dream big. The greatest innovations often start as bold ideas. Take the first step toward bringing your vision to life, whether through a startup, community project, or research initiative. Your contributions can lead to breakthroughs that change the world.

Conclusion

In conclusion, technology is a powerful force that can drive positive change in society. By engaging with these advancements thoughtfully and ethically, we can shape a better future for ourselves and generations to come. Let us embrace the spirit of innovation, harness the power of technology, and work together to create a world that thrives on creativity, collaboration, and progress. The future is not something we passively inherit; it is something we actively shape. With determination, curiosity, and a commitment to innovation, we can transform our ideas into realities that benefit humanity as a whole.

ACKNOWLEDGMENTS

In writing a book that seeks to inspire and inform, it is vital to acknowledge the many individuals and groups whose contributions have made this work possible. This section serves as a heartfelt expression of gratitude to those who have supported the author on their journey:

- **Mentors and Educators**: First and foremost, I would like to extend my deepest thanks to my mentors and educators. Their guidance and encouragement have shaped my understanding of technology and its potential to drive societal change. They have challenged me to think critically, engage deeply, and cultivate a passion for innovation that I hope resonates throughout this book.
- **Family and Friends**: A special acknowledgment goes to my family and friends for their unwavering support. Their patience during countless hours of research and writing was invaluable. They believed in my vision, providing the emotional support necessary to overcome challenges along the way. Thank you for your love, encouragement, and understanding during this journey.
- **Experts and Contributors**: I am grateful to the experts and professionals who generously shared their knowledge and insights. Interviews and discussions with leaders in technology, education, and innovation have enriched the content of this book. Their perspectives have provided clarity and depth, making the discussions on emerging technologies not only informative but also engaging.
- **Readers and Young Innovators**: Lastly, I would like to express my gratitude to the readers—especially young

innovators and aspiring entrepreneurs. Your curiosity, creativity, and passion for learning inspire me daily. It is my hope that this book serves as a source of motivation and guidance as you embark on your journeys to make a difference in the world through technology.

ABOUT THE AUTHOR

Er. Sandeep Chavan is a mechanical engineering graduate with over 22 years of experience in the fields of industry and education. His journey began in the manufacturing sector, where he honed his skills as an industrial engineer, working with top-class multinational corporations. Throughout his career, Sandeep has embraced the transformative power of technology, recognizing its potential to drive positive change in society.

With a passion for teaching, Sandeep has spent the last 13 years educating students in Physics, Chemistry, and Mathematics. His commitment to nurturing young minds has led him to empower students to think critically, creatively, and innovatively. Sandeep believes in the importance of fostering a culture of innovation and entrepreneurship among the youth, encouraging them to pursue their dreams and make a difference in the world.

As an advocate for ethical technology, Sandeep aims to inspire the next generation to approach innovation responsibly, considering the implications of their ideas on society and the environment. This book, "What Really Changed The World: Miracles of Human Intelligence," is a culmination of his experiences and insights, intended to inspire young innovators to explore the possibilities that technology offers and to equip them with the knowledge to shape a better future.

Sandeep is also an author of articles focusing on various aspects of technology and its impact on society. His writing reflects his belief that knowledge and innovation are the keys to unlocking human potential. He currently resides in India, where he continues to engage with students, educators, and entrepreneurs in his quest to promote technological advancement and ethical innovation.

REFERENCES

Books

1. **Kurzweil, R.** (2005). *The Singularity Is Near: When Humans Transcend Biology*. Viking.
2. **Marr, B.** (2018). *Data Strategy: How to Profit from a World of Big Data, Analytics and the Internet of Things*. Kogan Page.
3. **Tapscott, D., & Tapscott, A.** (2016). *Blockchain Revolution: How the Technology Behind Bitcoin Is Changing Money, Business, and the World*. Penguin.
4. **Gonzalez, R., & Woods, R.** (2018). *Digital Image Processing*. Pearson.
5. **Rifkin, J.** (2011). *The Third Industrial Revolution: How Lateral Power Is Transforming Energy, the Economy, and the World*. Palgrave Macmillan.

Articles and Journals

6. **Marr, B.** (2019). Artificial Intelligence: The 5 Biggest Opportunities in 2020. *Forbes*. Retrieved from Forbes
7. **Wright, A.** (2020). How 3D Printing is Changing Manufacturing. *MIT Technology Review*. Retrieved from MIT Technology Review
8. **Khan, M.** (2021). The Future of Augmented Reality: Trends to Watch. *Journal of Augmented and Virtual Reality*, 15(2), 23-34.
9. **He, H., & Wu, D.** (2020). Cybersecurity Challenges in the Age of AI. *Cybersecurity*, 2(1), 1-10.

Websites

10. **International Energy Agency.** (2020). Renewables 2020. Retrieved from IEA
11. **NASA.** (2021). The Journey to Mars: NASA's Vision for

Human Exploration of the Red Planet. Retrieved from NASA

12. **World Economic Forum.** (2021). The Global Risks Report 2021. Retrieved from WEF

Reports

13. **McKinsey & Company.** (2020). The Future of Work: Reskilling and Remote Work. Retrieved from *https://www.mckinsey.com/*

14. **Deloitte.** (2021). Technology, Media, and Telecommunications Predictions. Retrieved from *https://www.deloitte.com/*

MESSAGE TO READERS

Dear Readers,

As we navigate the complex landscape of our modern world, I want to share some reflections on the relationship between technology, human intelligence, and our potential.

We are endowed with an extraordinary capacity for creativity and innovation. From the invention of the wheel to the rise of artificial intelligence, our journey has been marked by remarkable advancements that have transformed our society and improved our lives. This power to reason, imagine, and create is nothing short of miraculous.

Yet, we must also recognize the paradox that accompanies this gift. While our intelligence enables us to achieve incredible feats, it also exposes us to the darker aspects of our nature. Throughout history, our innovations have been misused, leading to suffering and destruction. The very technologies that empower us can, in the wrong hands, become instruments of oppression and harm.

As we move forward in this age of rapid technological advancement, we stand at a critical juncture. We can choose to harness our capabilities for the greater good, creating a sustainable, equitable, and just future, or we can allow fear, greed, and ignorance to dictate our path.

I urge you to embrace a mindset of collaboration over competition, compassion over indifference, and integrity over profit. Let us engage in conversations that unite us in a common purpose: the betterment of humanity. Imagine a world where technology bridges divides, enhances our lives, and heals our planet.

This vision is within our reach, but it requires us to confront the truths of our nature. We must be vigilant stewards of our creations and continuously question the implications of our innovations. By inspiring the next generation to wield their intelligence for the greater good, we can foster a future defined by hope and responsibility.

Together, let us forge a path that reflects the best of human intelligence and counters the darker tendencies that threaten our progress.

Thank you for being a part of this journey.

Warm regards,
Er. Sandeep Chavan

BOOKS BY THIS AUTHOR

IT'S NOT AI, IT'S AHI - AMPLIFIED HUMAN INTELLIGENCE

It's Not Just AI, It's AHI: The Amplified Human Intelligence by Er. Sandeep Chavan offers a deep dive into the future of artificial intelligence, focusing on how AI can amplify human intelligence (AHI) to enhance our lives and potential. This book moves beyond the sensationalism of AI as a threat or autonomous entity, instead framing AI as a tool for amplifying human capabilities across industries and everyday life.

THE DECISION PARADOX: COMPLEX JOURNEY OF DECISIONS OUT OF CHOICES

In "The Decision Paradox: Complex Journey of Decisions out of Choices," Er Sandeep Chavan offers a compelling exploration of how modern individuals face increasingly complex decisions in everyday life. This book aims to unravel the layers of confusion that often accompany the decision-making process, helping readers to take control of their choices with greater confidence and clarity.

IGNORE WISELY: MASTERING THE ART OF SELECTIVE ATTENTION

Ignore Wisely: Mastering the Art of Selective Attention is a transformative guide designed to help readers regain control over their lives in an age of information overload, constant distractions, and unnecessary stress. In this book, the author explores how selective attention and intentional ignorance can significantly impact personal and professional growth.

THE IIT DREAM - IS IT WORTH IT?

The Indian Institutes of Technology (IITs) are often viewed as the pinnacle of engineering education in India, attracting thousands of students with dreams of academic excellence, prestigious placements, and global recognition. But is the "IIT Dream" really worth the hype? In The IIT Dream—Is It Worth It?, author Er. Sandeep Chavan seeks to demystify the journey to IIT, providing readers with an unbiased, comprehensive guide to understanding what IITs truly offer and what it takes to succeed there.

PREPARING FOR THE FUTURE: TRANSITIONING INTO HIGH-GROWTH TECH CAREERS

In today's rapidly evolving technological landscape, the future of work is becoming more unpredictable, yet full of opportunities for those willing to adapt and learn. "Preparing for the Future: Transitioning into High-Growth Tech Careers" by Er. Sandeep Chavan, addresses this critical transition period, offering valuable insights into how the tech industry is shifting and what professionals need to do to stay ahead.

www.ingramcontent.com/pod-product-compliance
Lightning Source LLC
Chambersburg PA
CBHW050320230526
45471CB00005B/2272